Bradt

Slow
New Forest

Local, characterful ~~guide~~ ~~special places~~

D0861327

Emily Laurence Baker

Edition 1

Bradt Travel Guides Ltd, UK
The Globe Pequot Press Inc, USA

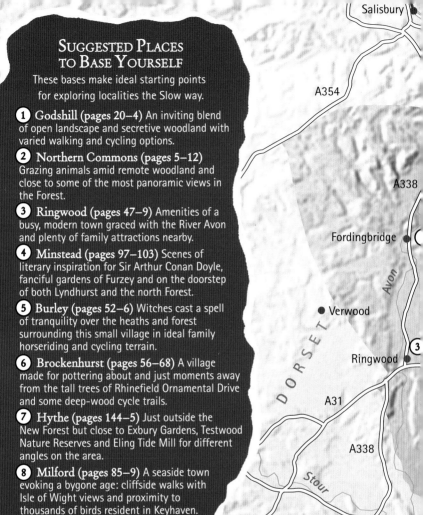

SUGGESTED PLACES TO BASE YOURSELF

These bases make ideal starting points for exploring localities the Slow way.

1 Godshill (pages 20–4) An inviting blend of open landscape and secretive woodland with varied walking and cycling options.

2 Northern Commons (pages 5–12) Grazing animals amid remote woodland and close to some of the most panoramic views in the Forest.

3 Ringwood (pages 47–9) Amenities of a busy, modern town graced with the River Avon and plenty of family attractions nearby.

4 Minstead (pages 97–103) Scenes of literary inspiration for Sir Arthur Conan Doyle, fanciful gardens of Furzey and on the doorstep of both Lyndhurst and the north Forest.

5 Burley (pages 52–6) Witches cast a spell of tranquility over the heaths and forest surrounding this small village in ideal family horseriding and cycling terrain.

6 Brockenhurst (pages 56–68) A village made for pottering about and just moments away from the tall trees of Rhinefield Ornamental Drive and some deep-wood cycle trails.

7 Hythe (pages 144–5) Just outside the New Forest but close to Exbury Gardens, Testwood Nature Reserves and Eling Tide Mill for different angles on the area.

8 Milford (pages 85–9) A seaside town evoking a bygone age: cliffside walks with Isle of Wight views and proximity to thousands of birds resident in Keyhaven.

9 Lymington (pages 77–84) A Saturday market, quayside crabbing, and a harbour crammed with yachts.

10 Buckler's Hard (pages 132–6) Quiet country lanes, Beaulieu River cruises and walks and a wealth of World War II and maritime history.

Salisbury

A354

A338

Fordingbridge

Avon

Verwood

DORSET

Ringwood

A31

A338

Stour

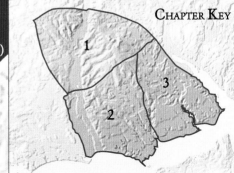

CHAPTER KEY

1

2

3

Romsey

A36

A31

Test

Itchen

A31

2

Totton

Southampton

4

Lyndhurst

A326

7

Hythe

A35

A337

B3054

Fawley

Burley

5

Brockenhurst

6

Beaulieu

10

Buckler's Hard

New Milton

9 Lymington

Christchurch

8

Milford on Sea

ngistbury Head

𝒩

Yarmouth

The Solent

Isle of Wight

0   5 miles
0   8km

A New Forest Gallery

Birdwatching is well rewarded at Keyhaven which is on the migration path of millions of coastal birds. (ELB)

Remnants of World War II airstrips make intriguing cycle trails through windswept Beaulieu Heath, where ponies wander freely. (ELB)

The animals that frequently halt traffic are a reminder that we humans are not always in charge. (ELB)

Walks in the northwest Forest include varied terrain of woodland and open heath as in this trail near Ogdens Purlieu. The hilliness in this part of the Forest provides views over woodland patches and beyond towards Wiltshire and Dorset. (SS)

You don't need to own a horse to enjoy the extensive trails throughout the New Forest. Numerous stables cater to all abilities, while accommodation with stabling is available for those who travel with their horse. (FC)

It's well worth slowing down to appreciate the smaller details that are easily missed. Martin Down National Nature Reserve is home to many butterfly species and wildflowers. (LS/NE)

Taking it Slow in the New Forest

The New Forest, where roaming animals regularly stop traffic, is made for taking it Slow. The best ways to explore are on foot, cycle or horseback and the numerous trails across heaths and through woodland make it easy.

Roydon Woods are within the New Forest National Park but its relative seclusion makes it seem like a different world. A walk here includes a bird serenade and a possible glimpse of deer in the dense canopy of trees. (ELB)

The countryside
Despite its relatively small size, the New Forest National Park has varied landscapes of open heath, dense forest, hills and valleys.

Nearly half of the New Forest is open land, as in this expanse at Rockford Common, prompting many visitors to ask 'Where actually is the Forest?'. (HH/ShS)

Longslade Bottom, near Brockenhurst, is a particularly inviting starting point for a walk or ride. The top of the hill gives far-reaching views, while in the valley the disused railway line provides an easily managed cycle path. (ELB)

The quintessential New Forest blossoms are gorse and heather, mainstays in the diet of grazing ponies. Gorse heralds the arrival of spring with its bright yellow flowers while vibrant purple heathers take over in summer. A guided walk with a ranger is the ideal method of slowing down and getting a closer look. (ELB and M)

The River Avon passes through the north and west Forest providing excellent fishing and riverside walking routes. (ELB)

The village of Buckler's Hard is rich in maritime and World War II history. (BEL)

Witches cast a friendly spell on the tiny village of Burley, where ponies wander along the main streets. (ELB)

Cycling and walking on roads within the Forest provide opportunity to see daily life unfold. (ELB)

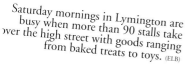

Saturday mornings in Lymington are busy when more than 90 stalls take over the high street with goods ranging from baked treats to toys. (ELB)

Home to Furzey Gardens, Minstead is an inspiring place to visit. (ELB)

At Vinegar Hill B&B you can spend the weekend spinning a potter's wheel and walking along the cliffs of Milford on Sea. (VH)

Rural life and community

Forest villages and towns are small but each has a distinctive personality worth seeking out. This little corner of Britain also packs in a notable concentration of history important to the nation.

Fordingbridge is named for the medieval Great Bridge with seven arches that span the River Avon in the centre of town. (SS)

The mosaic of habitats within the New Forest enables many varieties of bird to thrive, from waders along the coast to ground-nesting birds of the heathlands, like this Dartford warbler. (DM/FLPA)

Blashford Lakes Nature Reserve is the winter hideaway for thousands of waterfowl escaping colder northern climes. The reserve has excellent family programmes that encourage children to get close to wildlife. (BC)

Wildlife

From tiny insects and flowers to hulking Highland cattle that roam the Forest in summer, the New Forest has a fascinating array of foliage and creatures.

Brimstone butterflies are plentiful in the New Forest in summer but in order to see one you need to go Slow and wait patiently in a lightly wooded area. (FC)

Deer can be hard to spot in their native woodland but you are guaranteed a good view on a deer safari in Burley. (ELB)

Pigs are let loose in the Forest during pannage, a six- to eight-week period in autumn. The swine happily munch their way through thousands of acorns that can be poisonous to ponies. (DM/FLPA)

Open days at the Countryside Education Trust near Beaulieu, are an excellent way to experience rural life with activities including the opportunity to interact with farm animals. (CET)

The best features of a New Forest walk are the roaming animals which graze freely in all areas. These ponies at Hinchelsea, outside Brockenhurst, are a fairly sure sighting; ponies don't wander too far from their home ground. (ELB)

The costumed guides at Beaulieu Abbey make it easy to imagine the thriving community of monks who lived here during the 13th century. (NMM)

Sir Arthur Conan Doyle's final resting place in Minstead churchyard is much visited by Sherlock Holmes fans. (ELB)

Despite its grand exterior, Breamore House is a welcoming and intimate home with an historic Great Hall. In the grounds, the Countryside Museum, the impressive Saxon church and Breamore Mizmaze are fascinating accompaniments. (ELB)

The ancient craft of coppicing, in which trees are cut to promote continuous new growth, is still practised in the New Forest. Coppiced woodlands can be seen in numerous inclosures including Pondhead and Sloden. (FC)

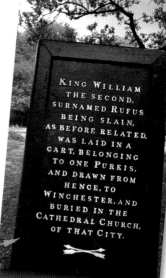

KING WILLIAM THE SECOND, SURNAMED RUFUS BEING SLAIN, AS BEFORE RELATED, WAS LAID IN A CART, BELONGING TO ONE PURKIS, AND DRAWN FROM HENCE, TO WINCHESTER, AND BURIED IN THE CATHEDRAL CHURCH, OF THAT CITY.

The Rufus Stone is one of the most-visited locations in the national park. But is the memorial in the correct place? (SS)

History and heritage

The New Forest harbours a wealth of historic remains, including Bronze Age barrows, the majestic arches of Beaulieu Abbey and craters from a World War II bomb testing site at Ashley Walk.

Thatched houses are plentiful in the New Forest. You can go inside a restored 16th-century thatched cob cottage at Furzey Gardens in Minstead. (SS)

Eling Tide Mill is one of the only tidal mills in the world still producing flour regularly. (MK/ShS)

The walk down to Lymington Quay from the town centre features colourful cottages, a cobbled street and plenty of ice cream stops. (SS)

You don't have to visit Hurst Castle to walk on Hurst Spit which has fantastic views of the Solent and Isle of Wight, as well as being a bracing fishing spot. (ELB)

From the wide cliffs of Barton on Sea, a path runs to Milford, where the 60-mile Solent Way continues to Emsworth, on the border of West Sussex. (SS)

The shingle beach at Milford on Sea is a perfect place for a summer day. (SS)

The coast

The southern border of the New Forest National Park is the Solent Coast where there are unspoilt coastal walks, wildlife reserves, and recreational boating and fishing sheltered by the Isle of Wight.

Birdwatchers come from all over the world to view wildlife at Lymington-Keyhaven Nature Reserve which also contains remains of the Lymington salt works. (BG/FLPA)

The tidy pathways and brilliant blooms of Exbury Gardens, just outside the New Forest, make a delightful contrast to the wild Forest landscape. (CR)

Gardens

From the grand layouts at Exbury to more simple designs of smaller patches, the New Forest has some pleasing formal gardens to visit.

Lunch or afternoon tea at The Secret Garden in Brockenhurst is a treat to be savoured at leisure. (ELB)

Fairy doors, thatched structures and other whimsical features grace the enchanting Furzey Gardens in Minstead. (ELB)

Author

American-born **Emily Laurence Baker** has lived in England for 22 years, dividing her time between London and the New Forest. Her articles on numerous topics have been published in *The New York Times*, the *Financial Times*, *The Wall Street Journal Europe*, *The Washington Post*, *The Guardian*, the *Daily Telegraph*, the *Sunday Times*, *Psychologies* and many other publications. She's also written the London edition of *City Walks with Kids* for Chronicle Books and an app for Sutro Media entitled *London Family Travel*. Her website is www.emilylaurencebaker.com.

Author's story

I didn't love the Forest when I first moved here. I had hoped to live on the coast but couldn't find anything suitable. The house search gradually moved inland and my husband and I fell hopelessly in love with a cob cottage (which I later realised was akin to living in a sandcastle), where ponies poke their heads over the gate to see if there is anything better on our side and cows plod past on their way to the heath for a drink.

When I began to write this book I realised that I had been living on the Forest's periphery for eight years – emotionally anyway. I rushed to work, rushed to children's activities, rush, rush, right on past the glories of this extraordinary landscape. As much as I enjoyed cycling and walking deep in the woods and out in the windy heaths, and the animals that stop traffic and meander down the high street, I didn't truly love the Forest until I understood its complexities.

I couldn't begin to love this land until I got to know the people who maintain it, those whose passion for the Forest and understanding of its origins help keep it as magical as when the earliest commoners grazed their animals here. Only when I understood the intricacies of this 'mosaic of habitats' as the professionals call it, could I fully appreciate how remarkable the diversity is within this relatively small area. You can still find yourself alone in the silence of woodland, heath or saltmarshes. I'm so glad to live in a place where I'm often forced to stop because a herd of cows has convened in the middle of the road.

First published April 2013
Bradt Travel Guides Ltd
IDC House, The Vale, Chalfont St Peter, Bucks SL9 9RZ, England
www.bradtguides.com
Print edition published in the USA by The Globe Pequot Press Inc,
PO Box 480, Guilford, Connecticut 06437-0480

ISBN: 978 1 84162 448 8 (print)
e-ISBN: 978 1 84162 759 5 (e-pub)
e-ISBN: 978 1 84162 661 1 (mobi)

British Library Cataloguing in Publication Data
A catalogue record for this book is available from the British Library

Front cover artwork Neil Gower (www.neilgower.com)
Illustrations Gary Long

Photographs
Emily Laurence Baker (ELB); Beaulieu Enterprises Ltd (BEL); Bob Chapman,
Hampshire & Isle of Wight Wildlife Trust (BC); Countryside Education Trust
(CET); Crown Copyright, Forestry Commission (FC); FLPA: Bob Gibbons (BG/
FLPA), Derek Middleton/FLPA (DM/FLPA); Mooburnes (M); National Motor
Museum, Beaulieu (NMM); Colin Roberts (CR); Lucy Rogers/Vinegar Hill Pottery
& B&B (VH); ShutterStock: Helen Hotson (HH/ShS), Martin Kemp (MK/ShS);
Linda Smith/Natural England (LS/NE); SuperStock (SS)

Maps Chris Lane (*www.artinfusion.co.uk*)

Typeset from the author's disc by Chris Lane, Artinfusion
Production managed by Jellyfish Print Solutions; printed in India
Digital conversion by the Firsty Group

Acknowledgements

I've been so impressed with the passion people feel for the Forest and I thank them for sharing their personal views with me. I hope I have conveyed their messages accurately. A few special acknowledgements to those who really made a difference, beginning with my family: Shu-Ming who made the whole thing possible on so many levels; to Zoe for endless encouragement; and to Quinlan for putting up with my extended absence. A huge thank you to John Jordan and Les Bowden, my first friends in the Forest and still my favourites; Andy Shore and Dave Dibden for showing me I live too fast; Henry Cole for his warm welcome and wealth of knowledge; Richard Reeves for perspective and humour; Suzie Moore; Jane Pownall for her inspirational work; Barry Dowsett (thanks for waiting); David Bridges for a delightful excursion; Neil and Pauline McCulloch; Sarah Hunt; Sue Palma; Andrea Finn; Alexis Scott-Thompson for her patience; Libby Burke and Hilary Makin for supreme efficiency; Claire Sherwood for sparing me the rain; Tom Hordle for restoring my faith in the next generation; Sarah Oakley; Paul and Mandy Manning for an outstanding adventure; James White for his generosity; Paul and Stephanie Callcutt; James Golding for his infectious enthusiasm; Dylan Everett for reading recommendations; Michelle Baxter; Jane Mills; Nick and Jackie Hull; Colin Turner; Ian Thew; Nigel Philpott; Debbie Mulkern; Pete White; Jonathan Gerrelli; Clive Maton; Robert Maton; Sally Fear; Diane Rayner; Susan Tomkins; Steve Marshall; Pete Durnell; Mike and Judy Smales; Sue Randall; and an enormous thank you to the meticulous Tim Locke for extreme patience and for making me better.

$$\bowtie$$

Illustrator: Gary Long Gary Long is an artist and illustrator based in Cornwall who has also been a part-time lecturer at University College Falmouth. His work is exhibited in the UK and the USA. More information can be found on his website www.garylongart.com.

CONTENTS

GOING SLOW IN THE NEW FOREST

The Slow mindset

Hilary Bradt, Founder, Bradt Travel Guides

We shall not cease from exploration
And the end of all our exploring
Will be to arrive where we started
And know the place for the first time.
T S Eliot 'Little Gidding', *Four Quartets*

This series evolved, slowly, from a Bradt editorial meeting when we started to explore ideas for guides to our favourite country – Great Britain. We wanted to get away from the usual 'top sights' formula and encourage our authors to bring out the nuances and local differences that make up a sense of place – such things as food, building styles, nature, geology, or local people and what makes them tick. Our aim was to create a series that celebrates the present, focusing on sustainable tourism, rather than taking a nostalgic wallow in the past.

So without our realising it at the time, we had defined 'Slow Travel', or at least our concept of it. For the beauty of the Slow movement is that there is no fixed definition; we adapt the philosophy to fit our individual needs and aspirations. Thus Carl Honoré, author of *In Praise of Slow*, writes: 'The Slow Movement is a cultural revolution against the notion that faster is always better. It's not about doing everything at a snail's pace, it's about seeking to do everything at the right speed. Savouring the hours and minutes rather than just counting them. Doing everything as well as possible, instead of as fast as possible. It's about quality over quantity in everything from work to food to parenting.' And travel.

So take time to explore. Don't rush it, get to know an area – and the people who live there – and you'll be as delighted as the authors by what you find.

With the free-roaming animals often halting traffic on Forest roads, the New Forest is almost 'Slow' by definition. It's not a big area, and savouring it slowly is the best way to appreciate its many distinctive qualities. The main things to do in the Forest are Slow in character: walking, cycling, horseriding, birdwatching – at the risk of sounding trite, it's all about nature. Even most of the attractions highlighted here relate in some way to natural surroundings. It's an easy place literally to walk off the beaten path. There are so many trails throughout the Forest and it doesn't really matter if you veer off one and aren't quite sure where you are. My happiest hours have been when I don't know where I am and have discovered a new corner of the Forest that subsequently becomes a favourite spot.

That said, the Forest can be disorientating. Anyone doing serious walking should have an Ordnance Survey Explorer map OL22 and a good pair of boots. Dry ground in the New Forest can quickly become a sodden mass or thick mud; this is not the place to walk in sandals or delicate trainers.

As much as the book is designed to help newcomers enjoy the Forest, I hope its contents will inspire residents and regular visitors to look beneath the surface of this remarkable location. It wasn't until I started writing this book that I began to take the guided walks offered by numerous organisations and realised how much I'd been missing and how little I really knew about the Forest.

Specialised walks can make the perfect introduction to the Forest. I am not a birdwatcher and was intimidated by my first birdwatching foray when everyone turned up in khaki gear with binoculars strapped to their belts. But in the Slow sense, there is no better way to see the Forest than standing quietly in hopes of spotting a rare winged creature. 'Most of us don't have time to walk this slowly through the Forest, and you wouldn't do it if you weren't here for this purpose,' said a fellow participant on a bird walk. Instead of stomping across heathland, I learned to look from the ground up by examining tiny flowers on the edge of paths or gently lifting bracken to be rewarded with a bright pink wild orchid. During a walk on one topic, you learn a surprising amount about all aspects of the Forest because everything is interdependent.

I was fortunate to spend time with many people whose families have been here for generations. They are at one with the Forest, partly because it is almost in their blood but also because they pass through slowly. Andy Shore, the Forest keeper at Bolderwood said it best: 'As soon as you move fast, you miss things. If you're in a car, you see less than if you're on a bike. If you're on a bike, you see less than if you walk.' I suspect that he would add that you ought to just stand still every so often, stand still and listen to the Forest around you.

The New Forest National Park

The New Forest encompasses about 92,000 acres and the national park is slightly larger. This is Britain's smallest national park but also the most densely populated. Some 34,000 people live within its boundaries, which stretch from the edge of the Wiltshire chalk downs in the north, to the Solent coast in the south, to the Avon Valley in the west, and on to Southampton Water in the east. Towns are within its confines, as are

Useful websites

Forestry Commission (*www.forestry.gov.uk/newforest*) All-encompassing. Has guided walks and visitor information, including campsites and history.
New Forest District Council (*www.thenewforest.co.uk*) Commercially orientated, with current events and online accommodation booking.
New Forest National Park Authority (*www.newforestnpa.gov.uk*) Excellent for general background.
New Forest Volunteer Rangers (*www.newforestvrs.org.uk*) Highly informative and has a slightly different take on Forest issues.

Additionally, *The New Forest* quarterly publication is available in tourist information centres and various outlets around the Forest and has good listings of current events.

remote heathland and woodland. This book doesn't stick to the park exclusively but strays a few miles beyond it where appropriate.

One day as I walked across the windswept expanse of Beaulieu Heath, located well within the New Forest border, a group of walkers stopped me and asked where the New Forest was. I was, of course, puzzled until I realised that they expected to find a giant woodland and their definition of 'forest' didn't include the great swatches of grassy lawn, heath and bog from which they had just extricated themselves. 'New Forest' is a misnomer in modern terms. There are, of course, woodlands – both ancient and ornamental – which are comprised of oak, beech, and holly, as well as conifer inclosures planted largely for timber harvesting.

The term 'forest', however, dates from a time when the word meant something else altogether. When William the Conqueror claimed this area for his private hunting ground in 1079 (his boundaries were in fact larger) the word 'forest' meant tracts of land reserved for the king and his barons to hunt rather than wooded land. 'New' is a relative description, but to William it was his personal 'Nova Foresta'.

What the Beaulieu Heath walkers didn't realise is that only 23% of the Forest is woodland in the modern sense of the word. Nearly 50% of the Forest is termed 'open forest', meaning unenclosed woodland, bogs and wet heath; heathland and lawn. The co-existence of these very rare habitats is extremely unusual and fosters a huge diversity of species.

But the New Forest's distinction doesn't stop there. This is also one of the last places where pastoral management, meaning the exercising of 'common rights' of animal grazing to maintain the landscape, continues. The ponies and cattle that wander the land are more than just a pretty rural feature; they, and the commoners who own them, work to keep the open Forest as it is for the rest of us to enjoy. The grazing practices here ensure that a complex network of natural habitats thrives. Nothing like this exists on such a large scale anywhere else in western Europe.

Perhaps the most prized feature of the Forest is that the public is, by and large, free to wander. The 134 car parks managed by the Forestry Commission are free and convenient for the huge number of walking trails (beware that parking on verges or in front of gates is likely to result in a ticket). Minimal signage is deliberate in an effort to maintain the natural appearance of the area. But that 'hands-off' management style gives visitors extra responsibilities. The Forest is a working environment, for commoners tending their stock, animals grazing the land, conservationists protecting rare habitats of flora and fauna, and for harvesters of timber, all of whom need to be treated with respect.

The people of the Forest are as important as its natural wonders. My conversations with those who live and breathe this landscape are included in this book in the hope that readers' experiences will be enriched and that they will be inspired to protect and care for this extraordinary place.

A New Forest miscellany

Here I include a selection of Forest cameos to set the scene about what makes this area exceptional.

Commoning

'When I was young, all we wanted to do was ride out in the Forest and work with our ponies,' said Clive Maton, a commoner whose family has been turning out ponies and cows to the Forest for 70 years. 'But now young people don't want to work with their hands anymore; they can make more money working with computers or whatever.'

This ancient system of land management is as old as the Forest and the rights of common even pre-date William the Conqueror's afforestation. By the time William the Conqueror established his private hunting ground in 1079, commoners were long here, happily managing the land in their own way. They have been facing newcomers ever since, now droves of them, due the Forest's proximity to London and accessibility from other part of the UK.

Commoning rights are granted to a property, not a person. Certain homes within the Forest (and some outside) hold these ancient rights to graze ponies and cattle, and in some cases sheep, in the Forest. To turn out animals, a commoner must have enough back-up grazing land for when stock needs to be removed from the Forest, as when animals are ill or when there is a national incident like foot and mouth disease.

The practice is not financially viable as a full-time living, except for some running very large farms. Most commoners are employed in other jobs, many working for the Forestry Commission, and continue to graze animals in order to retain the tradition and social core of this very private community, and of course to maintain the Forest. Consider the dedication involved: many commoners manage their animals in their spare time, some after working at an unrelated job. The fact that 80% of stock is owned by 10% of commoners shows how tenuous this existence has become.

Outside forces threaten this ancient form of land management, mainly the large number of visitors to the Forest and the rise in housing prices, driven by holiday home owners and retirees who perceive the Forest as a place for recreation rather than a working environment. When people buy homes with commoning rights and choose not to exercise them or perceive their grazing animals as pets, the system begins to break down.

But Clive and others are optimistic. 'The situation isn't as bad now as it was a few years ago.' He cited recent initiatives, particularly a Higher Level Stewardship scheme that has bolstered the commoning community. Other programmes are in place to make it easier for commoners to build houses, which will hopefully offset the rise in land and house prices in the area.

Clive has an unusual perspective in that he is not only a long-time commoner but a Verderer (see page 105) and is employed by the National Park Authority. Like many Forest workers, he believes that investment and commitment to the Forest has improved with National Park designation and that 'conservation measures actually support commoners' needs.'

Many people credit the stubbornness and tenacity that seems to be an integral personality trait of commoners for their survival. 'They don't like change and they'll fight to keep everything the way it always has been,' said one senior Forest manager. 'But that's precisely the quality that keeps the system going.'

Rights of common practised today

Some ancient privileges that are attached to certain properties in the Forest, like **marl**, which once allowed commoners to dig clay rich in fossil shells to improve soil, are no longer practised. The rights most likely to be exercised today are:

Estovers While this is technically the right to take firewood from the Forest, these days commoners with this right are provided with stacks of firewood from Forestry Commission timber plantations.
Pannage Also known as the right of mast, this is the right to turn pigs out on to the open Forest during the pannage season in autumn.
Pasture The right to graze livestock, usually ponies and cattle, on the

open Forest. Some properties also have the right to graze pigs and/or sheep.

Guardians of the Forest: the Agisters

'People visit the Forest and think that it's just here, on its own, existing all by itself. In fact there is a whole system at work with commoning at the core,' Jonathan Gerrelli, head Agister and foreman to a team of five, told me. 'One of the biggest misconceptions about the Forest is that the animals you see on the heaths and among gorse bushes are wild. They are in the sense that they graze the land but they all belong to someone and are carefully looked after.'

Agisters are the guys you see in Land Rovers or on horseback patrolling the Forest. Their job is to assist commoners, people with rights to keep animals on the open Forest, in looking after their 'stock', primarily ponies, cows and donkeys. They are appointed and employed by Verderers, members of the ancient court that protect their rights and with other groups who oversee the management of the Forest.

Agisters know the Forest intimately because their daily remit is to comb the land and look out for ponies and cattle that need assistance or to be moved because of changing land conditions. These people are on-call all day, every day, which can mean being called out in the middle of the night for an emergency, usually a pony that has been hit by a car.

Born in the Forest, Jonathan keeps cattle and ponies, as do all Agisters. Like all commoners, he is concerned about the future. Rising land prices, a growing number of outsiders settling in the area, and increasingly diverse user interest groups in the Forest all threaten this ancient system of land management. As visitor numbers have steadily increased, much of Jonathan's job now is liaising with the public. His easy-going charm and ability to deal with all types of people makes him a good ambassador but you can't help but think that he's happiest out in the Forest working with animals and commoners.

One of the busiest times of year is autumn when stock is rounded up. Ponies are herded into pounds located around the Forest where Agisters check the ponies' health and worm them, and brand any foals that are to remain in the Forest. They also collect marking fees from commoners and cut the tails of ponies to indicate that fees have been paid. The procedure derives from a medieval custom when fees were collected from 'strangers' who wanted to graze animals but had no right to do so. Agisters also have the authority to ask a commoner to remove a pony that they feel at any time of year is unhealthy. The animal is then taken from the Forest until it is deemed well enough to return.

The romantic notion of the Agister riding around on his horse all day saving the Forest isn't completely true to life. There is a lot of paperwork involved and a number of unexpected surprises. 'Often I'll plan to go out on my horse and examine the stock and the land and then the phone goes with someone telling me there is a mare stuck in a ditch or someone needs help rounding up cattle', said Jonathan. 'But that's one of the things I really like about my job – I never know exactly what the day holds.'

And when he does finally get out on his horse to make the rounds, the frustrations of the job balance out with the joys. 'When I'm riding out across the Forest and I see a bunch of ponies, that's when I think I'm lucky to get paid to do what I love.'

Ponies

Since medieval times, ponies have grazed the Forest, and still appear in certain villages. Two things about the Forest's 4,500 ponies need to be clarified. First of all they aren't horses. And secondly, they aren't wild; all ponies are owned by commoners (see page ix). When you see what seems to be a well-mowed grassy lawn, it's actually that way because ponies very helpfully tidy the grass and keep brush growth under control in the open Forest.

New Forest ponies are by nature sociable and mild-mannered. But sometimes their peaceful existence is threatened by humans who mean well by stroking them or feeding them when in fact these actions can lead to their removal from the Forest.

'The worst thing a visitor can do is feed a pony and yet it happens all the time,' said Jonathan Gerrelli, head Agister and one of the five responsible for looking after commoners' stock. 'Ponies learn quickly that humans mean an easy source of food. So by the end of the summer, they may approach people and possibly become aggressive in pursuit of a snack. Then visitors complain and that pony may have to be removed from the Forest.' As tempting as it is to approach them, the kindest action is to leave them alone.

Some ponies wander and graze freely in the Forest for their whole lives. Others are used for breeding or sold at auction (see page 110) to become family riding ponies. Efforts to 'improve' the breed were undertaken hundreds of years ago and continue today. 'We maintain quality of breeding by only allowing ten stallions out during breeding season from April to July,' explained Jonathan. 'The stallions are then rotated every three to four years.'

After years serving as 'architects of the Forest,' ponies have adapted to their environment with rough tongues that enable them to eat a prickly winter diet of heather and gorse, a surefootedness to dance across mires and bogs, and a hardy constitution to stand out in wind, rain and cold without the blankets worn by their paddocked cousins.

An uneasy balance: tourism and the Forest

There is a lot of disagreement within the New Forest about how land should be managed, how to control recreational users, and the implementation of environmental initiatives. But the one sentiment that is uniformly echoed among Forest leaders and commoners is that the greatest threat to the Forest's survival is tourists.

'The huge number of people who come to enjoy the Forest may unwittingly destroy the very landscape they have come to see,' said Jonathan Gerrelli, head Agister. It is not just the 13 million people who come here each year, which is maximum capacity now, but also the ways in which they interfere. 'Visitors don't realise how one seemingly innocent action can undermine the whole system at work. A commoner can spend three hours rounding up cattle and someone comes along with their dog which divides them, and there goes a whole half-day work. For those who do this in addition to a nine-to-five job, that's especially frustrating.'

Jonathan and other Forest leaders believe that the Forest is not robust enough to cope with all the user interests that make demands on the landscape. 'One cyclist may not understand why it's a problem if he rides on unmarked trails, but he fails to consider that there are many more cyclists right behind him and the extreme numbers will ultimately damage the Forest irrevocably.'

There is no simple approach to tourist management and possible ideas range from charging in car parks to taxing campers or building in a voluntary donation to hotel bills. But any solutions to limiting visitor numbers are complicated by the fact that so many people live within National Park boundaries and require unlimited access. At some point, certain areas may be designated for particular pursuits. 'Although it's wonderful to have so many people enjoying the Forest, visitors need to understand that this is a working forest and not just a playground.'

Who is in charge

Anyone who has spent even a little bit of time in the Forest quickly realises that it can be a political hotbed. So many groups have a vested interest in this land that they often conflict and you'll hear a different perspective on the Forest depending on whom you talk to. It's very clear, however, that the many management groups all wish to preserve the Forest and the commoning system; the sticking points are usually in the details.

The National Park Authority (NPA) and the Forestry Commission are the most visible organisations but neither owns any land. The NPA is an umbrella organisation that has authority for planning. Although initially many groups were opposed to the addition of another layer of management when the Forest became a national park in 2005, increased funding from having National Park status has benefited commoners and preservation efforts.

The Forestry Commission manages about 50% of Forest land on behalf of the Crown. This traditionally meant overseeing commercial timber plantations but in more recent years the focus has turned to conservation. The Forestry Commission manages most car parks and some campgrounds, employs rangers and conservationists, and has an impressive group of volunteer rangers who undergo a strict selection and training process. Other major organisations that own and/or manage land include the National Trust, the Hampshire County Council and the Hampshire & Isle of Wight Wildlife Trust (HIWWT).

'All those conflicting interests help keep the Forest the way it is,' said Sue Randall, a volunteer ranger and commoner. 'It means that no one organisation is in charge and that nothing gets done too quickly.'

Was that a pig I saw?

It's odd enough to come to the New Forest for the first time and see ponies and donkeys at roadsides and in certain village streets, but there is nothing quite like the first time you encounter a pig snuffling around in the woods. Every year, for a short time in autumn, pigs are released in the Forest to munch on beech mast, chestnuts and most importantly acorns, which are poisonous to ponies and cattle. Pannage, as the practice is called, is one of the ancient rights of common affiliated with certain Forest properties.

'Pigs are put out where there are a lot of oak trees because this is where ponies are in most danger,' explained Robert Maton, Agister for the Brockenhurst area. 'They can eat a lot of acorns, and that helps the ponies.'

Verderers determine when pannage will begin and end depending on how heavy the acorn crop is in any given year; according to ancient law, it must be a minimum of 60 days. In years of heavy acorn fall, the pannage season is sometimes extended. The number of pigs put out ranges from 200 to 600 although that's a big decline from the 19th century when there would be as many as 5,000 or 6,000. The only place you see pigs all year round is near the Northern Commons, which were the original 'adjacent commons' of the New Forest and have slightly different guidelines.

When it comes time to rounding up pigs at the end of the season, it helps to know a bit about pig behaviour. 'Pigs don't rough it the way ponies do,' said Robert. 'After a day of foraging they like to find somewhere warm and cosy to sleep. If the owner lives on the Forest, the pigs often will go home to sleep and if not, they'll find an open barn or shelter.'

There have been stories in recent years about pigs behaving aggressively towards people. This is unlikely but not impossible. 'A sow with babies can be dangerous and very grumpy. Best just to treat them with respect and make a wide berth', suggests Robert.

Butts, bottoms and balls: a glossary

Sometimes it's hard to keep a straight face when reading a map of the New Forest. What follows is a brief guide to the meanings of some of the Forest's distinctive terms.

Agister Employed by the Verderers, the five Agisters are responsible for the welfare of New Forest ponies.

Balls Hills in the northwest of the Forest, as in Sandy Balls.

Bog More commonly called 'mire' now, although there is a slight distinction relative to the amount of peat contained.

Bottom A valley. Examples are Longslade Bottom near Sway and (yes, really) Slap Bottom at Burley.

Butt A Bronze Age barrow (burial mound).

Commons Defined areas of land that are subject to rights of common.

Commoner A person exercising rights of common attached to property where he/she lives.

Down Open heathland.

Furze An ancient term for an area of abundant gorse.

Hat A small area of woodland standing on its own, as in Little Standing Hat at Brockenhurst.

Purlieu Land on the edge of the Forest that was once included in the Royal Forest but later separated and is exempt from Forest law. Dibden Purlieu, once part of the ancient Forest, is now part of Hythe.

Shade A place where animals rest but not in a sheltered spot as you might think. Usually refers to hilltops and open places relatively free of flies.

Verderer Any of ten officials who look after commoners' rights and Forest land use.

Note that **AONB** stands for Area of Outstanding Natural Beauty.

Inclosure vs enclosure

Even people who have spent their entire lives in the Forest argue over what these terms mean. Very simply, **inclosures** are places fenced off from grazing animals to protect trees for commercial timber harvesting. They are almost always timber plantations managed by the Forestry Commission. **Enclosures** result when private landowners have secured permission to close off land from commoning rights.

Lidar: high-tech mole

Modern technology in the form of what is termed lidar has enabled archaeologists to see not only below ground but also underneath shrubs and trees. 'Up until now, records of archaeological features have been quite limited,' said Lawrence Shaw, the National Park Authority's heritage mapping and data officer. 'But the scope and quality of lidar data is fantastically accurate and detailed. We are building a brand new picture of the New Forest both in terms of ecological features and archaeological study from prehistory to World War II.'

Experts estimate that it would take 100 years to gain a full archaeological picture of New Forest history using traditional field survey techniques but with lidar, it could be done in about ten years. Lidar, which stands for Light Detection and Ranging, scans a pulsed lasar beam side to side from an airplane. The pulses bounce back from the ground and are received by detectors on the plane which measure the distance between the plane and the ground. It can 'see through' all but the most dense vegetation like holly and conifer plantations.

Researchers have been able to identify ancient trees, old river systems, scrub growth and erosion, as well as archaeological sites. In 2009, the National Park Authority and the Forestry Commission conducted a pilot survey in the north Forest between Godshill and Burley. More than 400 archaeological sites spanning four millennia of history were identified, as well as new information about the World War II practice bombing range at Ashley Cross. Since then, scanning has continued all across Crown lands.

Originally developed for submarine detection, lidar has also helped to ensure that ancient sites are not damaged during conservation work. Ancient earthworks and veteran trees can be identified before any groundwork begins. Lidar data will also be used as part of the National Park Authority's 'New Forest Remembers' World War II project and images will be available for the general public to download.

Alien invaders

'Himalayan balsam was introduced to Britain in the 19th century as a decorative plant in the gardens of grand homes,' said Catherine Chatters, New Forest Non-Native Plants Officer at the Hampshire & Isle of Wight Wildlife Trust, as she bent down to pull out a sample. 'Now it has invaded rivers and other waters throughout the New Forest to the detriment of native species.'

I joined Catherine and her loyal band of volunteers for a day's session of balsam pulling in a damp woodland beside the Passford Water, a tributary of the Lymington River. She posts work events on the HIWWT website (*www.hwt.org.uk*) as if it's a jolly outing not to be missed and incredibly, the volunteers come. 'It's a nice way to be out in the Forest and it's very sociable,' Catherine told me as she yanked up a scraggly stalk.

On that day, there were seven of us, all regulars except for me. The group, some of whom also volunteer for the Forestry Commission's Two Trees conservation team, were experienced and clearly devoted to Catherine and her mission to eliminate non-native species from the New Forest. 'Not only does balsam crowd out native species but there is also some research that suggests it secretes a chemical that prevents native species from growing. So it's important we get it out.'

The New Forest Non-Native Plants Project, which began in 2009 as a joint effort among the Hampshire & Isle of Wight Wildlife Trust and many other organisations, is making such good progress that the original three-year contract was renewed for another three years. Catherine's partner in eradication covers the Avon Valley.

As we bent and pulled, Catherine explained the logistics of her seemingly Sisyphean task. 'First I need to find where the non-native plants are, which isn't easy because I can't always access private land. So it's a lot of banging on doors, putting letters in boxes and then gaining the trust of landowners to come on to their land and remove the non-native species, which include Japanese knotweed, giant hogweed, American skunk cabbage and New Zealand pygmyweed. Then I need to recruit volunteers or in more complex cases, contractors who can go in and remove the plants.'

She never came up for air, nor for that matter, did any of her volunteers. Just eyes down, backs bent and pulling from the roots. Sometimes everyone went quiet and there were only the gentle chirps of birds in the woods and a satisfying squelching as the mud relinquished the balsam roots.

Catherine's cheerful nature must be part of the reason the project has been so productive. She is so knowledgeable and dedicated that I felt motivated to pull as many of these invaders as I could. 'The project has been successful because landowners are co-operative and volunteers are incredibly helpful. We've also nearly cleared the Beaulieu and Lymington rivers by systematically moving downstream so seeds can't spread. We don't move downstream until we finish upstream.'

By lunchtime, I and my aching back had had enough but I enjoyed being with new people, united in a common cause. And, despite aches and a stinging nettle rash, I was pleased I'd done my very little bit towards protecting the Forest.

Mires: lifelines of the Forest

'They are the unsung heroes of the Forest,' said Sarah Oakley, an ecologist for the Forestry Commission, as we surveyed an extensive stretch of mires at Denny Bog, near Beaulieu Road Station. 'Mires work like sponges and are critical to how water is stored and distributed throughout the Forest. But they are extremely fragile.'

The New Forest National Park has 75% of northwestern Europe's valley mires – areas of permanently waterlogged soil in shallow valley bottoms. Drainage and development has caused them to decline in other parts of England, making the New Forest one of the most important sites for this rare habitat. 'New Forest mires are among the most pristine in Europe but they too have shrunk in recent years,' said Sarah.

In an ideal state, water moves slowly through valley mires. When they become waterlogged, organic matter accumulates as peat. Many New Forest mires decreased in size after 1949 when ditches were dug to speed up drainage and, in theory, improve or create grazing lawns for stock. 'Unfortunately, even when you dig a drain further down in the valley, the damage goes back up into the mire. The water table is progressively lowered through the whole system by depriving it of water build-up,' explained Sarah.

Work is now underway in the Forest to nurse wetlands back to health by removing the eroded gullies and channels that are cutting back into mires, enabling water levels to be raised once more; reducing encroaching scrub on streamside lawns; and removing non-native plant species that clog waterways. Restoring streams to their natural curves is part of that scheme.

'The peat in these mires is thousands of years old,' explained Sarah. 'About 150 species can live here including sundews, bladderwort, bog myrtle and sphagnum moss, which holds water in the mire long after surrounding soil has dried out.'

Stories abound about people and animals getting stuck in bogs. Although infrequent, it does happen, more often to ponies than humans. When an animal wanders in, it can sink up to its neck. The Lyndhurst Fire Department even has a special crane to pull unfortunate animals from sticky situations. Although it's unlikely that a person will get stuck, this is one of the many reasons the National Park Authority urges people to remain on marked trails.

A sign of local quality: the New Forest Marque

'Local' has become such a buzzword that its meaning is often distorted but the New Forest Marque (*www.newforestproduce.co.uk*) is a genuine means of identifying local produce. It is a scheme supported by the National Park Authority to help local producers stand out in the marketplace.

In order to secure a marque, producers must meet stringent standards relevant to their specialty and their products must contain at least 25% of New Forest produce. Members include bakers and other food producers, craftsmen, butchers and farmers. Lodging and dining establishments also participate in the Marque scheme by buying and serving local produce from Marque members.

'Consumers often mistakenly believe they are buying local or free-range produce that due to loose labelling guidelines are not authentic,' said Sarah Hunt, New Forest Marque manager. 'When a buyer sees the marque, he or she knows this is a genuine New Forest product.'

When Forest fire is a good thing

It can be quite a shock to see fire spreading across heathland and disturbing to see the spindly black skeletons of gorse left behind, but controlled fires are a critical element of maintaining the New Forest. Every year between November and March, the Forestry Commission burns about 2–3% of heathlands with about ten controlled burns each day.

'If we didn't practise controlled burning, heathland would revert to scrubby woodland and we'd lose the fragile habitat that we're trying to maintain,' said Dave Morris, Open Forest Manager. Not only is burning essential for regenerating growth, it is also the main method of preventing birch and pine from taking hold.

'People get upset when they see the forest burning because they think we are destroying habitats haphazardly. But in fact there is a lengthy planning process that begins in the spring when we determine the next season's burning sites.' An area is deemed to be ready when emerging seedling trees of birch or pine appear, and when heather is getting to the end of its natural life cycle.

Controlled burning has been practised in the Forest for hundreds of years. It began as a means of clearing land but at some point commoners realised that regeneration was a by-product and produced a palatable food source for livestock. Now it's done on a roughly 25-year cycle which actually invites greater diversity of species at different stages of regrowth.

Like most other aspects of Forest management, controlled burning has been influenced by environmental awareness. 'We select sites to burn based on when certain species inhabit a particular area. We burn about ten acres at a time whereas 60 years ago, before we understood about creating diverse habitats, as much as 120 acres were burned at one time.'

The gentle art of fishing

'It's the chalk streams that make fishing in Hampshire so special,' said Ian Thew, founder of the New Forest Shooting and Fishing School. 'The purity of the water, the constant, year-round, water temperature and subsequent abundance of insect life encourage fish to breed and grow in abundance.'

Ian, who coaches both beginners and more experienced fishermen in game angling and fly fishing, recommends receiving instruction in this gentle art. He suggests that beginners try **Holbury Lakes Trout Fishery** (*01794 341619; www.holburylakes.co.uk.*), which has four well-stocked lakes and chalk stream fishing in the river Dun, or **Rockbourne Trout Fishery** (*01725 518603; www.rockbournetroutfishery.co.uk*), where there are six lakes set in 52 acres of woodland and pasture. The ultimate fishing day would be to hire a private guide, as they often have access to private waters.

Most fishing waters in and around the New Forest are privately owned so you generally need to have a permit from a local organisation for the type of fishing you wish to do. **Christchurch Angling Club** (*01202 480009; www.christchurchac.org.uk*) is an ideal starting point as the website lists all local tackle shops that sell day permits. **Moors Valley Country Park**, (*01425 470721; www.moors-valley.co.uk*) runs beginners' courses during the summer and school holidays and sells day tickets for its lake. Or you could hire your own private fishing island: **New Forest Water Park** (*01425 656868; www.newforestwaterpark. co.uk*) rents out a small island with a log cabin, caravan and shed. Before heading out for freshwater fishing, anyone over 12 will need to purchase a rod licence from the Environment Agency (*www.environment-agency. gov.uk*).

Sea fishing is somewhat simpler; no licence is required. Popular locations are at Hurst Spit and local beaches where you can stand and enjoy the scenery with your fishing rod. You can go out with guided fishing boats from Milford, Keyhaven and Lymington. The Lymington website (*www.lymington.org*) lists a directory of local captains. If you arrange something ahead, most boats will supply equipment.

Slow Forest fishing: an expert's view

By Ian Thew, founder of the New Forest Shooting and Fishing School (01425 403735; www.shootingandfishing.co.uk). Ian offers private fishing and shooting coaching for individuals or groups and for all abilities. He also is the author of From a New Forest Inclosure, *musings on life from his home deep within the Forest.*

The New Forest is a mecca for fishing, bound as it is in the east and west by two celebrated rivers and in the south by the sea; few other areas of

Great Britain offer the angler such variety. The Avon and the Test rivers begin life north of the Forest as crystal-clear, chalk streams that rush headlong down the country in their haste to reach the sea. By the time they get to the Forest, they have matured to mighty rivers that now take their time and flow at a more leisurely pace to their journeys' end. These rivers, together with the smaller Beaulieu and Lymington, both of which rise within the Forest, provide excellent fishing opportunities for the game angler who seeks that king of fish, the salmon or his humbler cousins, the sea trout, brown trout and grayling. For the coarse fishing enthusiast, these rivers abound with record-breaking pike, barbel, chub, perch and many other species.

Where there are rivers there will always be lakes and stillwater fisheries. The New Forest is no exception. Day-ticket permits can be obtained from a variety of locations which will provide such quarry as fat, rainbow trout for the fly fishing aficionado or monster carp for the coarse fishing enthusiast. And then are the sea and the tidal waterways where the fishing can be as diverse as hand-lining for crabs from Lymington quay, fly fishing for bass on the mouth of the Lymington River or beach casting for whatever comes along at Hurst Spit.

No matter where you chose to fish in the Forest: in the dappled shadows of Forest trees, beside the lush water meadows of the Avon, on the banks of a picturesque lake or even on samphire-covered saltmarshes you will enjoy a slow pastime in a distinct fishing region of Great Britain.

How this book is arranged

For the purposes of this book, there is no need to distinguish between the New Forest and the national park. Where 'forest' is capitalised, it refers to the New Forest. The three chapters split the New Forest directionally, roughly using the A31 and the A337 as divisions.

All business establishments included here have been selected by me; no charges have been made.

Maps

Each chapter begins with a map with **numbered stopping points** that correspond to numbered headings in the text. Bear in mind that the New Forest is relatively small so a listing in one chapter may only be a couple of miles from one in another chapter. The featured walks have maps accompanying them.

The best OS map for the Forest is the double-sided 1:25,000 scale map Explorer OL22 (showing field and woodland boundaries, among other walker-friendly information). Perversely you need four sheets of the smaller scale 1:50,000 Landranger series maps for the whole area: most of it, however, is on sheets 195 and 196, with the northernmost bits on sheets 184 and 185, but there's only a tiny bit on the latter.

Accommodation

Accommodation has been chosen with an eye to geography and because an outlet embodies the Slow philosophy, either in general atmosphere or because it embraces a 'green' ethos. Most B&Bs in the Forest charge about £80 per night for two people sharing a room. I've used that figure as an average and considered anything above to be expensive and anything well below as budget. Virtually every owner I talked to seemed willing to negotiate, especially off-season. There are last-minute opportunities for one-night stays even for establishments that claim a two-night minimum. Campsite rates can be deceptive in that each has different charges for what is considered 'extra'. Rates are often calculated on the basis of two people with additional charges for extra children and adults.

Food and drink

I've listed favourite pubs, tea rooms and places to eat, with a firm accent on places that serve local produce or are worth singling out for some other reason, such as intrinsic character.

Getting around

I'd like to encourage people to **visit without a car** but it can be difficult, particularly in the north Forest where public transport is virtually non-existent. Cycling, horseriding and walking are ideal methods of Slow travel.

The Forest's newest initiative is a fleet of two-seater electric vehicles (*www.brandnewforest.com*) available for hire at Brockenhurst Station. A few local hotels also own them. Some lodging establishments offer discounts to guests who arrive without a car. Businesses that participate in the **Green Leaf Tourism** scheme which promotes eco-friendly tourism are listed on the website of New Forest District Council (*www. newforest.gov.uk*).

Trains

Options for getting around by train are limited to services on the line between Bournemouth and Southampton. From Bournemouth the line goes through Hinton Admiral, New Milton and Sway, then cuts across the heart of the Forest through **Brockenhurst** (the main access point), **Beaulieu Road** (a good three miles northwest of Beaulieu, but well positioned for walks) and **Ashurst New Forest** (three miles northeast of Lyndhurst), before entering suburbia and Totton.

Within the Forest, the Lymington to Brockenhurst Community Rail Partnership runs a local train from Brockenhurst to the Isle of Wight ferry landing in **Lymington**.

Buses and coaches

Several initiatives are making it easier for people to get around within the Forest without a car. The open-topped hop-on, hop-off **New Forest Tour** bus (*www.thenewforesttour.info*) has two routes: the red route travels around the north and west and the green route covers the south and east areas. The tour bus runs from the end of June until mid-September with regular stopping points, including connections to public bus routes X6, X1, X2, 112 and Bluestar 6. If you buy your New Forest Tour ticket on the bus, public bus fare is free. The bus carries up to four bikes; you can take the train to Brockenhurst or Ashurst and ride to a cycle hire shop and explore without ever needing a car. In Brockenhurst, **Country Lanes** (*www.countrylanes.co.uk*) will arrange accommodation and luggage transfers and suggested itineraries so that you can get off the train in Brockenhurst and cycle off from there.

Three major bus companies provide travel to and around the south and west New Forest. **Bluestar** (*02380 618233; www.bluestarbus.co.uk*) operates services from Southampton to Lyndhurst, Brockenhurst and Lymington, as well as buses to Hythe, where you can catch service H3 to Calshot, at the mouth of Southampton Water. Wilts & Dorset, now rebranded as **More** (*0845 894 2469; www.morebus.co.uk*) operates buses X1 and X2 from Lymington to Bournemouth via New Milton and Christchurch and also the X3 which runs between Salisbury and Bournemouth, passing through Downton, Breamore, Fordingbridge and Ringwood. Rural routes cover Lymington, Boldre, Beaulieu, Hythe, Burley and Ringwood. **Salisbury Reds** (*0845 894 2469; www. salisburyreds.co.uk*) runs bus X7 from Salisbury through the Northern Commons area and into Southampton and also rural route 40 which passes through Downton, Breamore, Woodgreen and Fordingbridge.

National Express coaches stop at Lyndhurst, Lymington, Ringwood and elsewhere in the New Forest (*08705 808080; www.nationalexpress. com*).

Bus routes can change from one day to the next, so it's wise to check the websites before setting out.

Cycling

The New Forest has 100 miles of marked trails so in theory you can cover a lot of ground. Unfortunately, not all the trails are linked so to get from one area to another often involves riding on roads. It's frustrating but it has improved and continues to do so with new trail markings and maps (available at tourist information centres and bookshops) that show cycle routes as well as smaller roads. The greatest concentration of designated trails is in the central Forest around Brockenhurst, Burley and Lyndhurst. You may cycle on bridleways but not on footpaths.

Off-road cycling is a contentious issue in the Forest, mostly concerning organised events involving large groups because these often interfere with commoning work. There is sometimes conflict between off-road cyclists and horseriders and walkers but that's usually when cyclists ride aggressively through trails shared by various users. Hard-core off-road cycling in the traditional sense is frowned upon in the Forest; cyclists are expected to be gentle and respectful of the landscape. Cycling off marked routes can damage the Forest and possibly disrupt wildlife so it carries a maximum fine of £500.

If you're intimidated by cycling on your own, consider joining a guided tour. Various companies offer **organised excursions**. I joined Paul and Stephanie Callcutt of **UK Wild Adventures** (*www.ukwildadventures. com*), who run day trips from London that include train fare, bike rental and a guided tour. I met them at Brockenhurst station, and after hired bikes were sorted for participants, we set off on a one-day 20-mile tour of cycle routes and roadways around Brockenhurst and Lyndhurst. I am an experienced cyclist but enjoyed the sociability of the group and the comfort of knowing that if something went wrong, Paul and Stephanie would take care of it.

Below I've listed four rental options at key points in the Forest. Included with rentals are children's equipment, including tag-a-longs and baby seats, and a basic repair kit.

Cycle hire

AA Bike Hire Gosport Lane, Lyndhurst SO43 7BL ① 02380 283349 ⓦ www.aabikehirenewforest.co.uk. This 'one-man band cottage rental shop' has a small selection of family bikes. Slicker outlets have grown up around the longest running cycle-hire shop in the Forest but it's still the only one in Lyndhurst. Good for people who want a short ride for the day at a less expensive rate. No reservations taken so arrive early when the weather is good.

Country Lanes Brockenhurst railway station, SO42 7TW ① 01590 622627 ⓦ www.countrylanes.co.uk. A national chain that also offers cycling holidays. In the Forest, it distinguishes itself by renting Ghost Mountain bikes which retail at the higher end of the market. Maps designed by staff feature different length routes throughout the Forest that avoid main roads. Because the shop is located at the station, you can't avoid some main roads but it's a quick ride to the edge of the Forest. Book two to three days ahead in summer and during school holidays.

Forest Leisure Cycling The Cross, Burley BH24 4AB ① 01425 403584 ⓦ www.forestleisurecycling.co.uk. When you hire a bike at this full-service shop, you receive a map of nine guided trails that feature pubs, the deer sanctuary and Forest scenery. With over 200 Giant bikes, the stock is unlikely to run out but it's still wise to book ahead. Bikes will be delivered to accommodation, including campsites. Families are their main client base. It's quick access to the Forest from the shop in Burley Centre.

Sandy Balls Holiday Centre Godshill SP6 2JZ ① 01425 470721 ⓦ www.sandyballs.co.uk. Cycle rental within the holiday park has a variety of Trek mountain and road bikes. They also pride themselves on offering a top-end Raleigh power-assisted bike. The ten maps devised by staff feature routes for all abilities, including more difficult cycle trails through Cranborne Chase and other northwest areas. The cycle shop, which will do repairs, is located near the Hampton Ridge trail and other Forest routes.

Trax ① 07850 043259 ⓦ www.bikehirenewforest.co.uk. Delivers bikes to your accommodation.

Walking

There is plenty of scope for walking in the Forest, either on designated footpaths and bridleways or 'off-piste' through woodland and across open heath. While you don't have a lot of obvious landscape features such as defined summits to head for, there are many routes that have a blend of scenery – open heathland, forest plantation, natural woodland, villages and waterside for example. I feature in full detail some of my personal favourite routes in this book.

Of various organisations in the Forest offering **guided walks**, the **Forestry Commission** has the biggest programme (www.forestry.gov. uk/newforest), with walks usually led by a volunteer who is passionate and knowledgeable about the theme of the route. I also recommend introductory walks from the **National Park Authority** and the '**New Forest in a Nutshell**' walks sponsored by the New Forest Centre. Generally you will be charged a modest fee but many walks are free.

Some notable **long-distance paths** run near or through the New Forest. Much of the **Avon Valley Path**, a 34-mile walking route that runs from Salisbury to Christchurch following the course of the River Avon, is within the west and north New Forest. The path is divided into five sections which make ideal daytrips but it can be waterlogged or flooded from December to May. The sections through water meadows have an open, pastoral quality quite different from the New Forest itself and a walk from the Forest into the Avon Valley can be rewarded by some striking scenic contrasts. Further east, the **Solent Way** (*www. solentway.co.uk*) a 60-mile footpath linking Milford with Emsworth Harbour, near Portsmouth, passes along the eastern edge of the Forest. Breaking it into daytrip segments is a good way to visit many coastal highlights, including Hurst Castle, Buckler's Hard, Beaulieu and the village of Hythe.

Horseriding

Horseback is a nicely appropriate way of seeing the Forest. Stables throughout the Forest are adept at guiding first-time riders as well as the more experienced, and you'll soon find yourself in remote reaches of the Forest. Below is a sampling of stables that cater to all abilities.

Stables

Burley Manor Riding Stables Burley BH24 4BS ① 01425 403489

Ⓦ www.burleymanorridingstables.co.uk. Friendly, flexible stables that accommodate all abilities. Situated behind the Burley Manor Hotel with direct access to the Forest. Guided summer pub rides for experienced riders.

Burley Villa School of Riding New Milton BH25 5SH Ⓣ 01425 610278 Ⓦ www.burleyvilla.co.uk. The only stable in the Forest to offer Western riding for anyone over 12: this is riding in a wide saddle, which is easy to balance in and is an ideal way to ride if you've never been on a horse before. Kids' lessons offered in the arena.

Fir Tree Equestrian Centre Ogdens Ⓣ 01425 654744 Ⓦ www.fir-tree-farm.org.uk. This livery works in harmony with horses using Reiki treatments. Fir Tree offers lead-outs, lessons and hacking.

Ford Farm Stables Brockenhurst SO42 7TB Ⓣ 01590 623043 Ⓦ www.fordfarmstables.co.uk. Easy access to wide variety of Forest terrain and walking distance from Brockenhurst railway station.

Feedback request

There are only so many special places and aspects of New Forest life that you can focus on when limited by word counts and book length. We've done our best to include a good mix and to check facts but there are bound to be errors as well as inevitable omissions of really special places. If you send an email to info@bradtguides.com about changes to information in this book we will forward it to the author who may include it in a 'one-off update' on the Bradt website at www.bradtguides.com/guidebook-updates.html. You can also visit the website for updates to information in this guide.

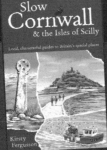
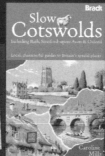
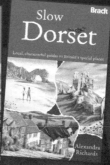

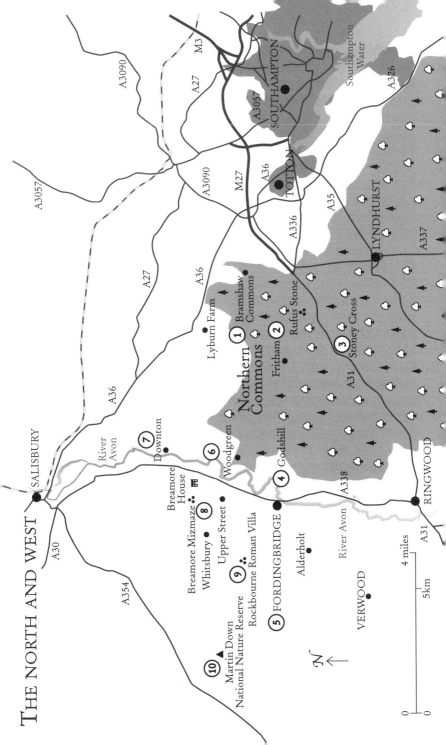

THE NORTH AND WEST

SALISBURY

A30

A354

A3057

A3090

A27

M3

M27

A27

A3090

A36

A36

A27

A36

A3090

A36

M27

A336

A336

A35

A3057

A36

SOUTHAMPTON

Southampton Water

TOTTON

A326

LYNDHURST

A337

RINGWOOD

A31

River Avon

River Avon

Downton

(7)

Lyburn Farm

Bramshaw Commons

(1)

Fritham

(2)

Rufus Stone

Stoney Cross

(3)

A31

A338

Northern Commons

Woodgreen

(6)

Godshill

(4)

Breamore House

Breamore Mizmaze

Whitsbury

(8)

Upper Street

Rockbourne Roman Villa

(9)

FORDINGBRIDGE

(5)

Alderholt

VERWOOD

Martin Down National Nature Reserve

(10)

N ←

0

0

4 miles

5km

⟨∼⟩ 1 ⟨∼⟩
THE NORTH AND WEST

Residents of the north Forest are protective of their quiet corner and rightly so. Fewer tourists come here than other parts of the Forest, largely because there are not as many attractions and you need to work a bit harder to get a feel for the landscape. Outdoor types are happy here – those who want to ride, cycle, fish, and most of all, walk. During an all-day trek you will be rewarded with varied terrain of rolling  hills, chalky and boggy ground, dark conifer woodland and the more dappled ancient and ornamental woodlands. There are also distant views of Wiltshire and Dorset farmland, quite a different backdrop from what you encounter in the central and southern Forest.

Cycling is particularly pleasant in the north Forest as roads tend to be quieter than in the south. **Hampton Ridge**, which cuts east–west through the Forest between Fritham and Frogham, is an ideal cycling path with views towards Dorset and Wiltshire. The area west of the A338 is not part of the national park but the quiet, hedged lanes around **Breamore** are peaceful and rewarding cycling territory. From here, it's not too far to **Cranborne Chase** where there are plenty of quiet roads through the Area of Outstanding Natural Beauty (AONB).

North Foresters are proud of their hilly topography; I've heard more than one speak disdainfully of the flatter landscape of Brockenhurst and coastal areas. It's certainly true that some of the choicest views in the entire Forest are here: **Piper's Wait**, at 422 feet, is the highest point in the Forest; **Stagbury Hill**, which has seven barrows and overlooks the northeast Forest; and **Bramshaw Telegraph** – such a good vantage point that it was the site of an optical shutter station that formed part of a signalling chain between Plymouth and London during the Napoleonic wars.

Accommodation

Alderholt Mill Sandleheath, Dorset SP6 1PU ℂ 01425 653130 Ⓦ www.alderholtmill.co.uk Ⓔ enquiries@alderholtmill.co.uk. A stream burbles and flowers bloom all around the red-brick mill house and adjacent cottages which offer average-priced B&B and self-catering accommodation. While the décor is a bit dated, the rooms are full of charm and very clean. Alderholt gets a lot of repeat business thanks to its congenial hosts and the superb breakfasts, cooked with local ingredients. The B&B has three doubles and one twin en suite plus a single with a separate private toilet and bathroom. There are three self-catering cottages; Miller's End and The Granary are spacious with beamed ceilings, while Mid-Mill has direct access to the garden (one week minimum in summer for the cottages but it's worth checking last minute). During weekend afternoons from Easter until August, the owners serve cream teas with scones made from the mill's flour and homemade jam. The mill is often working then and you can watch the flour being made. The house is right on the road but the garden, where you can barbecue meals, is quiet and peaceful. Private fishing available – bring your own tackle. No children under eight.

Bramble Hill Hotel Bramshaw SO43 7JG ℂ 023 8081 3165 Ⓦ www.bramblehill.co.uk Ⓔ bramblehill@hotmail.co.uk. A very unusual opportunity to stay in one of the Forest's original 18th-century Forest keeper's lodges. The hotel's old-fashioned flavour is surprisingly refreshing in an age of sleek mod-cons. Bedrooms are furnished with antiques and some have bay windows overlooking ancient woodlands. The huge house is a treasure, so if you fancy stepping back in time, this will delight. In spring and summer, the rhododendron-lined drive is a majestic entrance. You can even book a picnic in a vintage car and sip champagne while listening to a wind-up gramophone. Rates are more than the average B&B but lower than most hotels and include breakfast.

Bramshaw Forge Bramshaw SO43 7JB ⓣ 023 8081 3873
ⓦ www.bramshawforge.co.uk ⓔ enquiries@bramshawforge.co.uk. The
setting of this 18th-century forge and cottage B&B is idyllic, just by the
Northern Commons. Rooms are small but tidy and quiet. One double and
one small twin are in a cottage next to the owners' house and have their
own entrances. The Garden Room has its own private courtyard; the other
two rooms share a garden with barbecue. Continental breakfast is included
and brought to the rooms but cooked breakfast is £10 more, served in a
tiny dining room adjacent to the bedrooms. Rates are quite good with
just continental breakfast. It has an immaculate garden; no children. Open
Easter–November.

Furze Hill Cottage Furze Hill SP6 2PT ⓣ 01425 650581
ⓦ www.bedandbreakfastnewforest.org.uk. ⓔ rooms@
bedandbreakfastnewforest.org.uk. Not too many homes boast such a
postcard view beyond their garden gate. Well off the beaten track, this
guesthouse is situated on a dirt road. The prize double room is the Balcony
Room complete with tiny table overlooking the hills. The other double, the
East Room, is a larger en-suite room with a fireplace. Overflow guests can
use an additional twin room that shares the bathroom with the East Room.
Breakfast features fresh, warm rolls, eggs from the chickens that wander
freely in the garden and freshly squeezed orange juice. Staying here is like
visiting family; Lindsey and Michael will provide a picnic lunch and even
prepare dinner by request. You get better rates the longer you stay and three
nights in the Balcony room is a good deal.

North Gorley Tea Rooms North Gorley SP6 2PB ⓣ 01425 657628
ⓦ www.littlemere.com ⓔ info@littlemere.com. This restaurant with tea
rooms also has two small double rooms with an option for a connecting
single, which is handy and good value for families with children. Rooms
overlook the manicured garden and open on to an attractive tiled terrace.
Ideal if you want B&B rates (although there is small supplement for full
English) but the independence of a hotel. Breakfast is served on the outdoor
terrace or in the restaurant.

Red Shoot Camping Park Linwood BH24 3QT ⓣ 01425 473789 ⓦ www.
redshoot-campingpark.com ⓔ enquiries@redshoot-campingpark.com.
There's camping for tents, caravans and motor homes in a pretty field
behind the Red Shoot, a popular pub which brews its own ales and
welcomes children inside. It has 110 pitches in one main field with several
side fields separated by hedges. Dogs are welcome and it is very family
orientated – there is a children's play area and the small on-site shop stocks

as many toys as it does food. Unlike many New Forest campsites, Red Shoot has a cattle grid so you will not awaken to a curious cow poking her nose inside your tent. The shower block has underfloor heating and it's quiet at night though can get crowded at peak periods; laundry facilities are on site. Booking ahead is essential for one of the 45 pitches with electricity hook-ups. Reasonably priced.

Sandy Balls Godshill SP6 2JZ ① 0844 693 2949 ⓦ www.sandyballs.co.uk ⓔ post@sandyballs.co.uk. Jokes about the name aside, this family holiday centre has lodging to suit every budget from basic tent camping to fully-equipped wood-panelled lodges. The 120-acre site is like a mini village with a small grocery shop and restaurant. The premium cabins cost more than nearby self-catering accommodation but you get all the facilities which include beauty treatments, bike rental, a leisure centre with pool and indoor and outdoor children's activities. There are also rates for half-price board which includes a two-course dinner and breakfast. Less expensive units are very close together so would not suit people desiring a reclusive get-away but lots of fun for families looking for a sociable atmosphere.

Undercastle Cottage Woodgreen ① 01747 828170 ⓦ www.hideaways. co.uk (property number H211) ⓔ enq@hideaways.co.uk. An elegantly setup self-catering cottage surrounded by fields on the River Avon that gets booked up well ahead despite upmarket prices. The high-ceilinged, thatched, timber-frame house looks old but is a modern build that sleeps four in the main cottage plus up to eight in outbuildings. Guests can enjoy private fishing on half a mile of river and a rowing boat is available. The only downside (or up?) is that it is close to the busy A338, but when you're there it feels secluded.

North Forest: the Northern Commons, Fritham and Fordingbridge

You are constantly reminded of archaeology when visiting the northern and western regions of the New Forest and especially further west from Martin into **Cranborne Chase**. This chalk plateau that runs through Dorset, Hampshire and Wiltshire is where Augustus Pitt Rivers, considered to be a founding father of British archaeology, excavated ancient ruins on his private estate. Here I include a small corner of Cranborne Chase at **Martin Down**; for more on the area, see the Bradt guide, *Slow Dorset*.

While researching this book, I became enamoured with the watercolours of **Heywood Sumner**, an artist active in the Arts and Crafts movement, and who painted scenes conveying the stillness and beauty of the Forest that still prevails. As I delved deeper into the history of the north Forest, I learned that Sumner is best known for his archaeological contributions which, although not completely accurate regarding Bronze and Iron Age settlements, shed much light on Roman influence in the Forest. Now it seems impossible to me that someone could come to this part of the Forest and not appreciate the varied works of Sumner.

I leave it to this expressive artist and writer, who so deeply loved this landscape, to describe the riches of this region.

Here, on the Northern side . . . we have long rolling hills, capped with plateau gravel and clothed with heather, fern, and furze, worn into five parallel ridges and furrows by streams that trickle in dry, and rush in wet weather, down gravelly courses to the broad valley of the Avon. Here and there the hills are covered with thickets of holly, thorn, yew and crab-apple; with old woods of oak, beech, yew, holly, thorn and white-beam and with enclosures of Scots pine, larch, oak, and sweet chestnut. But the main features of our side of the New Forest are heather uplands, winding moorland streams, and scattered woods. The open country is never far distant.
Heywood Sumner *The Book of Gorley*

① Northern Commons

'This is how this land would have looked in the days before the private plantation was here,' said Dylan Everett of the National Trust, as we stood on a hill in the Northern Commons overlooking a panoramic display towards Southampton. 'This whole view has opened up since we removed conifers and birches.'

As the Trust's New Forest Operations Manager, Dylan is overseeing an enormous project at **Foxbury Plantation**, the Trust's most recent acquisition, to restore this former timber plantation to the open heathland that would have been here in the 19th century. The work here is reflective of a trend throughout the Forest, to reinstate lands as they originally were and allow native species to thrive.

The National Trust, the second largest landowner in the Forest, owns 3,300 acres of mostly 'adjacent commons,' traditionally privately owned lands that bordered the Forest but were not subject to its rules. They were brought into Forest borders as recently as 1964. Taken as a

In the footsteps of Heywood Sumner, artist and archaeologist

The west and north New Forest strongly influenced the works of Heywood Sumner (1853–1940), whose writings and drawings depict all aspects of Forest life vividly. Sumner was good at so many things and slots into no single category. He was a pioneer archaeologist whose recordings of excavations at New Forest Roman potteries paved the way for scholars behind him; a naturalist who painstakingly noted observations of wildlife and landscape as they changed seasonally; and an artist whose drawings and watercolours still evoke the serenity to be found during a walk deep in the woods. The combination of those attributes continues to provide unparalleled insight to the Forest.

A leading light in the Arts and Crafts movement, he worked as an artist in London designing tapestries, wallpapers and furniture, as well as illustrating books and crafting sgraffito murals and church stained-glass windows. He then moved to Bournemouth, allegedly because of his wife's ill health although the overriding factor might have been that he had tired of the London scene and sought a more tranquil existence. In any case, Bournemouth soon proved to be too suburban for his liking and he set his sights on a home in the Forest.

He built a house at Cuckoo Hill in Gorley and it was from here that Sumner began to make a name for himself as an archaeologist at sites in Cranborne Chase and the New Forest. The first archaeologist to scientifically investigate and record the New Forest potteries, he also discovered and excavated the first intact pottery kiln at Ashley Rails. What distinguished Sumner was his detailed analysis in which he identified which areas of the Forest pottery came from. Many artefacts he unearthed are kept at the Salisbury Museum. Meticulously, Sumner recorded his findings of storage pots, platters and bowls, along with educated conjecture about kilns and how the pottery was made. His archaeological notes were spiced with observations of Forest life and drawings that only someone who loved every aspect of the Forest could

whole, the Northern Commons – made up of Hale Purlieu, Bramshaw Commons (including Plaitford Common), Hightown Commons and, further west, Ibsley and Rockford Commons – present diverse landscapes. 'Ibsley and Rockford are pristine heathland sites while Hale

provide. I was lucky to retrace his routes around Fritham and through Sloden and Pitts Wood Inclosures with local historian Henry Cole; part of the walk is detailed on page 14.

Not surprisingly, Henry believes that Sumner would be disappointed in some elements of the Forest today. 'He would have been horrified at the number of people who visit the Forest and the number of cars. But he also would have been pleased that so many people want to look after the Forest and that there are so many restoration projects underway.' Henry also thinks that Sumner would have been thrilled by modern technologies like the use of ground-penetrating radar and lidar (see page xvi) for archaeological discoveries.

The artist went everywhere on his bike, possibly travelling as many as 60 miles a day, explained Henry. 'I can't help but think how exhausted he would have been to cycle on rough trails from Ibsley and then conduct excavation work when he got here.'

One of Sumner's greatest gifts to us was encouragement to leave the beaten track and explore out-of-the-way pockets of the Forest. 'Many of the views Heywood Sumner painted are similar today, although he did take liberties with moving things around to suit his ideal view,' said Henry, who has made countless excursions to the Forest to identify views that Sumner painted.

Heywood Sumner's original books are now out of print, but there are modern reprints still available. *Cuckoo Hill: The Book of Gorley*, a 1987 facsimile adaptation of Sumner's original three volumes, is highly readable and features beautiful watercolours of the north Forest. New Forest libraries have copies of most of his books in Local Studies reference sections, as does the Christopher Tower Reference Library in the New Forest Centre.

Henry Cole (07748 026230; henrycole@sky.com) is a local historian who lectures regularly on Heywood Sumner and New Forest airfields. He is available for guided walks and illustrated talks.

boasts a rich mosaic of habitats including dry and wet heath, mires and woodland, all of which are grazed by commoners' animals,' Dylan told me. 'Hightown, the smallest of our holdings, serves as an excellent gateway to the Forest because it's close to Ringwood. Bramshaw

A young commoner's perspective

'Keeping cattle has become quite challenging,' said Tom Hordle, as we climbed one of the hills that characterise Rockford Common in the west Forest. 'I have to file papers every time I move a cow, even if it's just a mile down the road. I need to keep medical records, have tuberculosis checks and maintain buildings.' But he insists that it's worth it because keeping cattle on the Forest is critical to its survival as we know it.

Tom, 22, is bucking trends. The number of young people who practise their rights to graze animals on the Forest is dropping. But as a full-scale commoner, he maintains the farming tradition that has underwritten the Forest since Anglo-Saxon Times. Fewer commoners now graze cattle on the open Forest but Tom is chipping away at those statistics too by turning out a small herd of cows which he plans to increase.

'Ponies and cattle graze differently and this ultimately will affect the composition of the landscape. Ponies nibble but cows graze deeper and eat rough plants like heather and tough grasses. If we lose too many cows, the large expanses of green lawns in the Forest could become overgrown.'

Commoning is under threat, so it's inspiring to see a spirited young man like Tom engaged in a life that was once routine in the Forest, especially since the time demands keep him from nights out with friends. 'I love it and I can't imagine doing anything else. My great-grandfather kept ponies in the Forest but neither my grandmother nor father chose to use the rights that are attached to our family home. When I was ten, I befriended a neighbour who kept cattle on the Forest. I used to go help him out after school and he taught me so much. He gave me my first cow when I was 11 and I still have her. She gives me a calf every year.'

Commons traditionally is a stronghold of livestock commoning, which you don't see to the same extent in all parts of the Forest.' Certainly if you walk through Bramshaw Commons, you are very likely to encounter cows munching their way across the acid grasslands that characterise this area.

Foxbury has retained some species that would have been here prior to the planting of the commercial plantation because land intermittently was cleared for use as a hunting estate over the years. The Trust is helping to re-establish them by nurturing a hospitable environment.

His pride was palpable as we stood atop the hill from where we could see towards Fordingbridge and beyond. 'They say that commoning is in your blood and I think that's true. Even though it skipped two generations, this is what I've always wanted to do.'

Tom works for the National Trust ('my day job') doing landscaping projects but as soon as he clocks off, he's busy tending his herd or helping his now elderly neighbour who believed in him from the start. 'It's a bit easier for me because I have an employer who understands the demands of my lifestyle. In an ordinary office job, which many commoners now have, the boss won't understand if you need to leave early to help birth a calf.'

Job commitment is just one of the obstacles Tom cited that keeps young people from pursuing this lifestyle. 'Land and house prices in the entire Forest area are prohibitive for someone like me. The grants and housing schemes now available help but there isn't enough for everyone.'

In addition to the housing issue, it's also hard to afford back-up grazing land for when stock needs to come off the Forest due to illness or supplementary feeding needs. 'Recreational horseriders are able to pay more for grazing land than we can so the balance of land use is tipping. The way people view the Forest has changed. Now most people don't rely on it – they just like to live in it.'

Not only has Forest use changed but its management has too. 'The Forest is now managed for conservation which on the whole is a good thing. But there are so many groups involved doing what we always have done anyway,' he said with a smile that reflected wisdom well beyond his years. Then he fixed his cap, whistled for his dog and headed back to his Land Rover to tackle another job on the Forest.

As we walked further into the emerging heathland, Dylan was visibly excited at the changes taking place: 'Already you can see new heather growth on the areas cleared first, which in turn will encourage the return of heathland species including nightjar and woodlark'.

Dylan pointed out rhododendron lining some of the paths. Consistent with work by the Forestry Commission and conservation groups elsewhere in the Forest, the Trust is trying to eliminate it from the Northern Commons because it can harbour disease that can kill oak and larch. 'Rhododendrons are not native to this area – they come from

From milk to cheese: changing with the times

Lyburn Farm Lyburn Rd, Landford, Salisbury SP5 2DN ① 01794 399982
Ⓦ www.lyburnfarm.co.uk.

Mike and Judy Smales have been farming on this northern tip of the New Forest since 1952. They decided to make cheese when the price of milk sunk so low that they were losing money on their dairy herd. They still produce milk because 'we have the infrastructure so it would be foolish not to continue,' said Mike from inside one of his barns as we waited for a rain shower to pass. But the cheese business has taken off and they now produce one tonne of it annually, in the form of Winchester, Stoney Cross, Lyburn Gold and others. All of their cheeses have won national and international awards. 'We knew when we started that we couldn't compete with the Cheddar market so we decided to create artisanal cheeses. Our niche is Old Winchester, a vegetarian, hard, crumbly cheese made similarly to a Gouda. It can be used for grating, as a substitute for Pecorino or Parmesan, both of which use an animal rennet.' Mike and his family seem to have found the right recipe because they are selling to Waitrose, Fortnum & Mason, farmers' markets and local shops throughout the south, as well as to the US.

The Smales also grow organic vegetables which they supply to box schemes Abel & Cole and Riverford.

the Himalayas. They were planted during the age of Capability Brown who believed in bringing colour to the Forest.' These dense plants also served as hiding places for pheasants during Victorian hunting parties.

'We'll never be finished here because the work is always evolving,' said Dylan. 'More important than looking at the timescale is making sure the work is done the right way, meaning restoring the land sustainably for the future. We need to determine grazing patterns that benefit restoration of the land and weigh the balance when one action might cause problems somewhere else.'

He cited the presence of **mires** throughout this land as an example. 'Mires are extremely valuable areas of wetland that host rare plant and animal life. The New Forest has some of the only remaining mires in western Europe so we obviously have to be careful when working around them. Sometimes removing a tree for one conservation objective isn't

A good time to visit Lyburn is during the annual Hampshire Food Festival. For a few evenings in July, Mike and his sons take visitors on a tour of the 450-acre farm in trailers attached to huge tractors. Seated on hay bales, you bounce along over the fields and learn about the challenges involved with growing organic vegetables. You'll get a close-up view of some of the 170 cows that produce 1.3 million litres of milk annually. And you're also likely to hear Mike pronounce on the doom that supermarkets, 'purveyors of mediocrity', bring to dairy farmers. 'When supermarkets reduce milk prices to such a large degree, producers can only operate at a loss,' Mike explained to our group. 'There needs to be more equal distribution among producers, processors and sellers.'

After the tractor ride, guests are treated to a cheese supper laid out on picnic tables. All food is truly local: bread from a nearby bakery, lettuce from Hayward farm 'down the road', Hill Farm apple juice, wines from Setley Ridge and courgette chutney made by Judy. It feels like a family supper on the farm.

Mike has chosen to bypass supermarkets by appealing to a 'small but discerning percentage of the market'. You can purchase Lyburn cheese at farm shops throughout the New Forest or at the small shop on the farm which is usually open weekdays around midday but it's best to call to be sure.

justified because we can only get it out by dragging it across a mire, and this can damage many species, as well as the mire itself.'

Because of the scale of tree felling here and other ongoing conservation work, **access** is restricted at Foxbury. There is a public right of way from Bramshaw Commons through to Bricky Lake Lane but areas off the main pathways are not open. The Trust holds regular **activity days**, some of which are dedicated to particular user groups, including horseriders, cyclists and walkers. There also are easy hour-long **walks with rangers** in which you can learn about the ongoing work. The rangers are friendly and passionate about their projects and the walks are an ideal way to gain understanding of the complex nature of conservation work. 'It's not as simple as just removing non-native species and opening up land,' explained Dylan. 'Conservation always is the primary consideration and that can be very complicated.'

Food and drink

Le Frog at Les Mirabelles Nomansland SP5 2BN ℗ 01794 390205
Ⓦ www.lesmirabelles.co.uk. An incongruous setting for a quietly
sophisticated French restaurant but a welcome treat in Nomansland. Yes,
the owner is French and the authentic food has been delighting Salisbury
and Forest residents for 18 years. Booking essential at weekends, as it's
very popular.

② Fritham

Walkers flock to Fritham, partly because refreshment at the **Royal
Oak**, one of the Forest's best-loved pubs, is a wonderful finish to a
walk, and partly because within a small area you can see a variety of
Forest landscapes. Although the village seems quiet today, in the late
19th century, Fritham was headquarters for the **Schultze Gunpowder
Factory**, which manufactured smokeless gunpowder popular with the
hunters of the day. The factory was probably established here because
of the remoteness of the site and also because black powder had been
manufactured here in the 1860s from the abundant charcoal in the
Forest.

The business began in three huts with transport conducted by just
one man and a wheelbarrow but grew to ultimately include 70 buildings
and employ about 100 workers. The transport system evolved from a
wheelbarrow, to horse and carriage, to cars. Wages were considerably
higher than for agricultural work, prompting some workers to walk
many miles daily for factory jobs.

Water from Eyeworth Pond, today a tranquil spot with water lilies
and waterfowl, was used to power factory machinery. The manmade
pond was completed in 1883.

Charcoal was not used in smokeless powder; the main ingredient was
wood pulp, which oddly did not come from New Forest trees. The
shavings were imported in prepared sheets which were then treated
with acids that made the wood an explosive compound. Obviously the
work was dangerous and there are reports of occasional explosions.

The factory boom was relatively short-lived and by the early 20th
century manufacture had ceased in this area. You can still see evidence
of the gunpowder heyday in addition to Eyeworth Pond: a blackened
letterbox at the edge of the car park; Powder Mill Road (now a cycle trail
which leads from Eyeworth Pond to the B3078), originally designed
so that dangerous substances wouldn't have to be ferried through the

village; and Eyeworth Lodge, initially a hunting lodge and later the research lab where Schultze's head chemist worked. Today it is a private home.

Lunch with history

Royal Oak Fritham SO43 7HJ ☎ 023 8081 2606. Not open all day; no credit cards.

'Meet me at the Royal Oak,' is a phrase used among Forest residents regularly and has been for hundreds of years. These days, it's hard to visit this 17th-century pub when it's not overflowing with people but there are moments, as when I met owners Pauline and Neil McCulloch one morning before lunch to chat about running this New Forest institution.

We sat in the middle room, behind the bar, which is known locally as the 'unofficial parliament of the New Forest' because it is rumoured to have served as a meeting point for Verderers and other Forest overseers. Neil and Pauline, who have run the pub since 1998, chuckled at the reference and admitted the link might be slightly exaggerated. 'That reputation probably originated from when they first began enclosing the Forest, much discussion took place here,' said Neil. 'And of course Verderers and Agisters come here but perhaps meetings aren't held to the degree it's been suggested.' He paused for a moment and considered. 'But actually, members of the New Forest Association were in last week, busy stuffing envelopes.' It's safe to say that the pub is a popular meeting point for those managing the Forest, those working in it, and those just enjoying it.

Running a pub is difficult enough but overseeing one that is steeped in history and expectations intensifies the challenge. On top of that, when the McCullochs took over, the Royal Oak had been run by the Taylor family for 90 years. 'Locals were worried that we would change it, that it wouldn't be the same place they'd been coming to,' said Pauline.

In order to maintain the Royal Oak's longstanding status as a nighttime watering hole, the McCullochs don't serve food in the evening. At midday, they offer only simple Forest food – no gastro-pub pretensions for this straightforward couple. Lunch consists of ploughmans, pork pies, their very popular smoked duck pâté and, in winter, homemade soup. And they don't do chips.

'Nearly every other pub in the Forest does chips and we're happy to direct people to one of them,' said Neil matter-of-factly. 'We don't serve chips because the thatched roof retains oil smells, not to mention the potential fire hazard, and also because it doesn't suit our menu of fresh, simple local food.'

That simplicity has served the pub well throughout its history. Even Heywood Sumner, the early 20th-century artist and chronicler of Forest life, advised his readers to take lunch there in a booklet published for the British Medical Association in 1934. 'From frequent experience, I can commend a bread and butter and cheese and beer lunch.'

As was a matter of course in Sumner's day but is now a trend, Neil and Pauline are dedicated to sourcing all food as locally as possible. 'We won't use any food or drink from more than 40 miles away,' said Neil, who was born in Lyndhurst. And for most ingredients, they do better than that. 'It's really not difficult to find everything we need within a few miles from here.'

Neil hopes to reduce those distances even more by turning his attention to the 55 acres of farmland that came with the pub. 'Up until now I've been focusing on the pub but I'm going to begin keeping cattle. Ideally we'd like to supply all our own pork.'

One of the most striking features of the Royal Oak is its diverse clientele, which includes tourists, walkers, businesspeople on their way home from work, and village regulars. That it has such huge appeal to such a diverse group is a real credit to the McCullochs and perhaps a nod to the charm and history that graces this small landmark. 'On any given night the crowd around the bar can include retired farm workers to judges,' said Neil.

Beer connoisseurs go out of their way to visit the Royal Oak for the outstanding selection of cask ales – up to seven at any time. 'It's beer in its purest form, straight from the barrel,' said Neil. One big change from the past is that there are many wines by the glass now, perhaps because Pauline has an eye for the female market. She's clearly proud that in this formerly male-dominated pub, women visit on their own now. 'They want clean glasses and cold white wine,' she said laughing. 'It's simple, really. Just keep it simple.'

A walk from Fritham through Sloden Inclosure: in the footsteps of Heywood Sumner
By Henry Cole, Forestry Commission volunteer ranger and local historian
This walk (which can be muddy and is not suitable for very young children) from the Forestry Commission car park at Fritham (grid

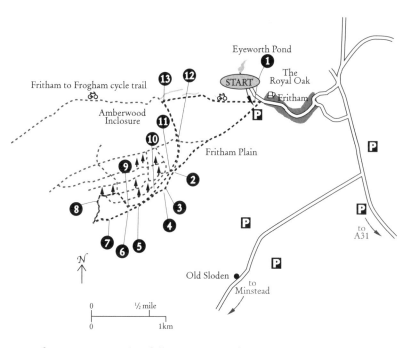

reference SU231141) follows a gravel forest road into the depths of Old Sloden wood, a route taken many times by Heywood Sumner in the period just before and after World War I. In distance the walk is five miles but covers around 3,000 years of history.

1 At the far end of the main car park take the gravel track heading out across open heathland (to the left of the 'Additional Car Park' sign). Ahead you will see a clump of small trees straddling the track. Pass through these trees and on your left after 110 yards in the bracken is a **Bronze Age barrow**. One of over 200 such burial mounds in the New Forest dating back around 3,000 years, the barrow has been excavated producing some cremation fragments and flint tools.

2 Just before you enter Old Sloden Wood, by an intersecting track on the right, you can detour into the trees on your left. There you will find the remains of a **World War II sawmill**. All that is left are the loading ramps and some lumps of concrete. This is one of several long forgotten sawmills located around the New Forest which played their part in the war effort. Venturing a little further back on the track you will see to your right the fence, banks and ditches of Sloden Inclosure, but more about that later.

❸ After 130 yards along the track you will see a grass track to your right. Before turning onto this path pause and look around you. You are on the very edge of **Old Sloden**, what Sumner described as 'the most beautiful wooded hillside . . . nowhere in the Forest do yews and whitebeams grow in such profusion'. Standing in the tranquillity of this setting it would not be impossible to imagine an elderly bearded gentleman dressed in tweeds cycling towards you ready for a day's archaeological investigation. Thankfully little has changed since Heywood Sumner's day. Now turn sharp right off the main track into the woods and carry on walking along a grassy track.

❹ In 65 yards, look carefully for a bank cutting across the path. This is the eastern edge of the **medieval coppice**. The practice of enclosing areas of woodland and renting them out by the Crown for coppicing goes back to medieval times. It was a very important source of revenue during the reigns of Henry VIII and Elizabeth I. In 1609, James I felt that he wasn't getting sufficient revenue from the 12 New Forest coppices and sent a well-known map-maker, John Norden, to survey them. Norden's remarkably accurate drawings match up perfectly with the coppice boundaries shown on today's 1:25,000 OS maps. The King's suspicions were well-founded and Norden reported back that the coppicers were carrying out 'an abuse intolerable'. Oak and beech were being cut as well as the permitted small trees.

❺ After strolling through this area of ancient and ornamental woodland (normally just referred to as A&O woodland) you will cross the western edge of the coppice bank after 550 yards. There is no precise definition of A&O woodland but it normally refers to unenclosed woods going back to the 18th century or earlier. The term was first used in the New Forest Act of 1877. Notice that many of the yews for which Sloden was famous are in poor condition; the cause of deterioration is unknown.

❻ With a fence on your right, follow the grassy path after crossing the coppice bank for 200 yards where you will cross the first side of small rectangular earthwork known as **the Churchyard**. Each side is about 47 yards long. Sumner surveyed it in 1915 after sketching it in 1913. He thought it was an animal enclosure but it is now believed to be one of at least six medieval hunting lodges built in the Forest. Continue along the grassy path, which runs along the top of a small ridge, and after a few yards you will see two massive pollarded ancient oaks (for more about pollarding, see page 60). We don't know how old these trees are but we can be certain that these two oaks were fairly mature in

1698, as that was the year when pollarding was made illegal by William III because the government required tall straight timber from maiden (unpollarded) trees for the Royal Navy.

7 Follow the path between the two oaks for 110 yards. You will emerge from the wood to enjoy what must be one of the finest views in the Forest. Looking ahead you can see right across to Ogdens and Abbotswell. The inclosure in the middle ground and slightly to the left is Hasley. On the far side of Hasley are humps and bumps of **quarrying work** carried out by the Roman-era potters. They needed lots of heath stone to make their kilns. On the nearer side is a track composed of red sand due to its high iron content. The 'red sands' are a favourite gallop for local horseriders as it is fairly soft if you fall off. The hill where you are standing is known as **Ragged Boys**. Sumner investigated local place names and believed that 'boys' was a corruption of the French 'bois' meaning wood – so a literal translation would be Ragged Wood.

Now descend the hill towards the gravel track. There is no defined path but it is an easy descent. On reaching the track turn right and head towards the inclosure.

8 Enter the inclosure through a gate and keep going straight on. Sumner described **Sloden Inclosure** as having been planted in 1864 with oak, ash and Scots pine with a few well-grown Douglas and Silver firs. The taller Douglas are probably the ones Sumner mentioned and are likely to be some of the first introduced to England by David Douglas in the first part of the 19th century. A short distance ahead, the track forms a T-junction. Turn right here and after 200 yards turn right again off the track (ignoring the first grassy turn-off on the right) and ascend up a fairly wide grassy path which begins gently and gets steeper back towards Old Sloden.

9 At the top of the path you will find a gate in the fence separating Sloden Inclosure from Sloden Wood. Go through the gate and turn left along the fence line, keeping the inclosure fence to your left.

10 Soon you will find come across a **large clearing** to your right. This is the site of one of the Roman potteries that Sumner excavated and recorded. To see what one looked like visit the New Forest Experience near Ringwood where there is a replica. The New Forest produced huge amounts of pottery between the late 3rd and late 4th centuries. The landscape must have looked very different from today with the area being covered with potters huts and kilns and small market gardens. Sumner investigated 17 kiln sites and plotted many more spoil heaps;

additional sites have been found in recent years.

Continue along the path and you will pass through a very well-defined section of the medieval coppice bank, then go forward towards where you originally entered the woods.

⓫ Just outside the edge of the woods rejoin the gravel track that you were on earlier and turn left on it. When you emerge into a clearing turn left again almost immediately and walk on the grass, keeping the fence of Sloden inclosure on your left. Cross over another gravel track, and opposite the vehicle access gate to the inclosure look for a well-worn track on your right that bears left away from the original gravel track. Continue straight on. After 550 yards through a mix of heather and gorse the track passes through a large group of very old hollies. A group such as this is known as a 'holm' locally.

⓬ At this point if you look to your left and right in the holly holm you will see an impressive **bank and ditch**, which is visible for two miles. Sumner believed that it was a demarcation boundary defining the pottery areas. It is worth exploring here for a little while and marvelling how these banks have survived for some 1,600 years.

Continue along this path. It is a bit rutted in places but a lovely varied part of the Forest. After 400 yards, you will enter **Crock Hill inclosure**. Sumner suspected the name derived from the large amount of very fine Roman pottery shards found in the area. After 220 yards, you will join the main track and cycle route from Fritham to Frogham.

⓭ Turn right on to the gravel track and follow it back towards Fritham. After 750 yards, you will see paddocks to your left. On the far side of the field is a **grassed-over mound** which is the last surviving blast-proof storage building from the gunpowder factory at Eyeworth. Follow the track a short distance back to the car park.

At the entrance to the car park look out for a small black postbox on your right. This was put up by the gunpowder factory so that the postman did not need to enter the works. This was probably not just for the benefit of the postman but more likely for the safety of the workers in case the postman was a smoker.

I hope you have enjoyed following in a few of the footsteps of George Heywood Manor Sumner, artist and archaeologist.

Henry Cole (07748 026230; henrycole@sky.com), a volunteer ranger with the Forestry Commission, lectures regularly on Heywood Sumner and New Forest Airfields to interested societies.

③ Stoney Cross

World War II temporarily transformed the peaceful Forest into a place of tense anticipation played out in the drone of airplanes and gathering of troops waiting to leave for the D-day invasions. Throughout the Forest, there is evidence of the huge role this area played in battle preparations, particularly at Lepe, Beaulieu, Ibsley, Stoney Cross and Ashley Walk, known then as Ashley Bombing Range.

The most visible wartime remnant at Stoney Cross (itself uncomfortably placed along the north side of the A31) is the road to Linwood, part of which was a 2,000-yard runway. The airfield here was used by both the Royal Air Force and the US Army Air Force. Other remainders are less obvious but the National Park Authority website has a downloadable audio tour in its 'Visiting' section which brings this piece of history to life (*www.newforestnpa.gov.uk*). Integrated with a tour of the hard-to-find wartime indicators, are recollections from personnel and people who lived in the area at the time. Near the end of the war, the Forest here was buzzing with planes regularly taking off and landing for missions. Local residents went on with daily life but listening to this soundtrack is a poignant reminder that the war deeply influenced Forest history. Former service roads have now been incorporated into the Ocknell and Longbeech campsites.

Aside from the wartime history and despite the relentless roar from the A31 dual carriageway that bisects the Forest, it's still worth visiting Stoney Cross for the sheer wildness and beauty. When you stand out on Stoney Cross today, the writing of John Wise in 1882 still makes sense:

> *If any one wishes to know the beauty of the Forest in autumn, let him see the view*
> *from the high ridge at Stoney-Cross. Here the air blows off the Wiltshire Downs finer*
> *and keener than anywhere else. Here, on all sides, stretch woods and moors. Here, in*
> *the latter end of August, the three heathers, one after another, cover every plain and*
> *holt with their crimson glory, mixed with the flashes of the dwarf furze.*
> John R Wise *The New Forest: Its History and its Scenery*

Rufus Stone

All is not what it seems at the Rufus Stone, one of the most visited sites in the Forest. The stone is real enough but the accompanying history and geography might be on dodgy ground. The story that is regularly repeated and that prompted the erection of the original stone in 1745, is that during a hunting expedition in 1100, William II, known as

William Rufus, was enjoying his hunting ground when his finest archer, Sir Walter Tyrell, aimed at a stag but the arrow ricocheted off an oak tree, striking the King in the chest and killing him immediately. The question of whether the incident was an accident or a deliberate plot to remove the unpopular monarch has long surrounded the tale.

In more recent years, debate has concerned the location of the event. Historians now believe that the present metal pillar, which encases the original stone, is on the wrong side of the Forest. Richard Reeves, librarian at the Christopher Tower Reference Library, thinks that the death took place at Truham, now known as Througham, on the Beaulieu Estate. So how did the monument end up near Fritham? 'It's possible that Truham was misidentified as Fritham and at some point Castle Malwood was brought into the myth as being the place where Rufus had stayed the night before his death.'

Richard, who knows a tremendous amount about New Forest history, thinks that there are other oft-repeated untruths. 'Most of the myth is wrong or confused. Rufus was probably hunting from Brockenhurst and not Castle Malwood, which is an Iron Age hillfort, not a medieval castle. Even his death is confused as I believe there are no fewer than four ways he died, according to the chroniclers.'

So go along and visit this memorial but do so to stir your interest in history, not because you are standing where it really happened. Fortunately it's lovely to walk among the many oak trees here, possibly relatives of the long-gone oak that might have caused Rufus' demise.

The easiest way to reach the Rufus Stone is from the B3078, heading right at the Bell Inn at Brook. The Stone is about a mile after the Sir Walter Tyrrell pub on the right.

⊙ Godshill and around

The Godshill area is a good base for exploring the north Forest. The difference in landscape between the flat, boggy heathland in the south Forest and the wide vistas visible from the ridges and hilltops of the north Forest is readily apparent in the many walking trails carved out here. The stretch of the B3078 from Bramshaw Telegraph along Deadman Hill and on to Godshill is one of the prettiest roads in the Forest.

The choice of walking and cycling possibilities include **Hampton Ridge**, a five-mile trail with some of the best views in the entire Forest;

Maintaining an ancient tradition

Godshill Pottery Godshill SP6 2LN ℗ 01425 657115 ⓦ www.
katecharmanartist.co.uk.

Kate Charman and her husband, Chris, have been producing pottery at this small roadside studio ever since electricity was installed here in 1964. They make simple, traditional earthenware and stoneware plates, cups and decorative pieces, all of which are decorated by hand. Everything is made on site, with clay from their own pit mixed with Devon clay which enables them to fire it hot enough to make domestic pottery.

Time stands still when you visit the studio. Signs direct you to the showrooms, the walls of which creak and bend with the temperature or wind. You can wander on your own and when you're ready to purchase or ask a question, just ring a bell and someone will greet you.

There are two galleries displaying pottery, and a smaller one with Kate's paintings of the New Forest. Although she has spent much of her artistic life working with textiles and pottery, her deepest love is painting. 'My New Forest scenes are inspired by the many years I've spent riding, walking and cycling through the Forest and observing the changing landscape.'

it runs between Fritham and Frogham with pubs usefully placed at either end. **Bike hire** is available at Sandy Balls (*www.sandyballs.co.uk; see page 4*), a family holiday centre near to where the off-road cycle trail begins at Abbots Well. The trail runs along Hampton Ridge all the way to Fritham (about five miles) where you can have lunch at The Royal Oak (see page 13). You have choice views along the route, although it can be windy, and can easily extend it by using the quiet roads around Fritham. Going the other way, the Forester's Arms is half a mile from the start of the bike trail.

World War II history abounds in this area. Inert bombs were tested throughout **Ashley Walk** and some traces can be seen, although much has disappeared. The bombing range was constructed in 1940 when animals were removed from a 5,000-acre tract of land , which was fenced off. You can still see concrete directional signals near Deadman's Hill on the Godshill to Cadnam road and concrete light boxes at various points near Hampton Ridge. The most easily located wartime evidence is near

Hampton Ridge outside Pitts Wood where you can see what are known as the **Sub Pens** (or Submarine Pens), and other wartime scars. These are detailed in the walk on page 23.

Food and drink

Fighting Cocks Godshill SP6 2LL ☏ 01425 656462 ⓦ www.fightingcocks pub.com. A jolly, lively pub popular with walkers and local families. Its child-friendliness means it can be mayhem on weekend early evenings and lunchtimes (there's a small play area). Better for drinks rather than meals.

Foresters Arms Frogham SP6 2JA ☏ 01425 652294 ⓦ www.theforestersarmsfrogham.co.uk. There's lots to look at in this good old-fashioned, red-walled pub with no music, just friendly conversation. It has a relatively small bar area but boasts a very local selection of real ales. Lots of dogs at lunchtime in the large garden.

Gorley Tea Rooms North Gorley SP6 2PB ☏ 01425 657628 ⓦ www.littlemere.com. When the weather is fine, this is a delightful spot for morning coffee or a light lunch at the tables overlooking the small garden. Open April–October only, closed Sunday.

Hyde Food Shed Hyde SP6 2QB ☏ 01425 652050 ⓦ www.hydegarden shop.co.uk. Part of the Hyde Garden Centre, this licensed tea room is a pleasant stopping point for refreshments if you're walking, cycling or just driving through the narrow country lanes of the northern Forest. Simple fare, friendly service, outdoor tables by the nursery. This is also a good place for breakfast.

Little Mere Restaurant North Gorley SP6 2PB ☏ 01425 657628 ⓦ www.littlemere.com. A hidden surprise frequented by locals. The conservatory with fairy lights or the outdoor garden terrace (site of Gorley Tea Rooms) make pleasant spots for a before-dinner drink and the tile-floored dining room with tall chairs is a cosy atmosphere for a leisurely meal. The menu changes regularly to make use of seasonal produce, prepared and presented to a high standard. Booking is recommended. Open Thursday–Sunday.

Three Lions Stuckton SP6 2HF ☏ 01425 652489 ⓦ www. thethreelionsrestaurant.co.uk. Stuck in a bit of a time warp, but a tasty one if you pine away for old-school French reductions done to perfection by Michelin-starred chef Mike Womersley. Most ingredients come from the Avon valley and New Forest. Expensive but reliable.

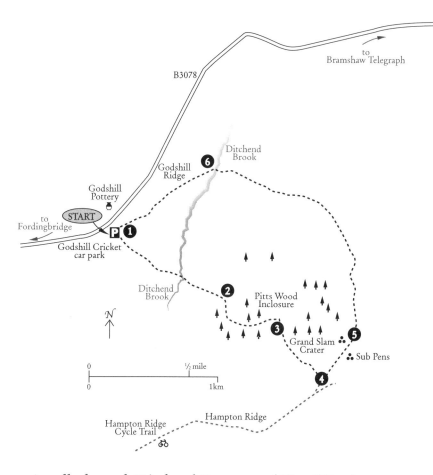

A walk through Ditchend Bottom and Pitts Wood inclosure

You have plenty of walking choices from Godshill. This three-mile route takes in a sampling of the valleys, conifer woodlands and wide vistas that characterise this area. Like many New Forest walks, this one can be very wet and you have to cross several streams so appropriate footwear is recommended. Look out for pillars that are remnants of when the woods were enclosed. Originally enclosed in 1775, Pitts Wood has been opened and closed several times since. Grid reference SU182151.

1 Begin at Godshill Cricket car park. With the car park behind you, keep to the right of the cricket ground, walking straight from the hut to the edge of the trail down to Ditchend Bottom. Cross two streams and follow a track straight into the woods.

❷ Follow the track uphill, veering left slightly to where it widens considerably. Do not follow the left fork but continue straight up the hill past another junction of tracks.

❸ About three-quarters of the way up, turn sharp right at three pillars, leaving the inclosure on a narrow, rough path. At the top of the hill, keep walking straight onto a wider track. You will pass a wide grassy track on your left, do not take this but keep straight on along another track, which curves slightly right.

❹ After 500 yards, turn left where a gravel track crosses (this may be waterlogged in places, but you can detour round any puddles). As you walk, you will see a large mound ahead to the right of the track. Walk 300 yards to it and climb up on one of the paths. This is known as the **Sub Pens**, a World War II bomb-testing structure. Climb down on the side facing Pitts Wood Inclosure and walk straight ahead and slightly left to see the **crater** from the ten-ton Grand Slam bomb which lies to the south of Pitts Wood. Resume the trail, heading right towards the southeast corner of the inclosure.

❺ Re-enter Pitts Wood in-between two pillars. Just past them on the right is a stone dedicated to Gerald Lascelles, a much lauded deputy surveyor of the Forest from 1880 to 1914. Follow the track down to the stream. Cross and continue up the hill on the other side. As you climb the hill, notice bricks in the path, leftover reinforcements from World War II. At the top of the hill where you emerge into the open air, follow the track straight on. Another track joins from the right, continue straight as the track passes through a small cluster of trees and downhill towards Ditchend Book.

❻ Turn sharp left after a bridge (the main track continues uphill towards Ashley Walk car park) onto a rough path that alternates between grass, sand and gravel. Rise to the opposite side of the cricket ground where you started.

⑤ Fordingbridge

Named after the medieval bridge with seven arches that majestically crosses the Avon, Fordingbridge is officially a New Forest town but with the added flavours of Wiltshire and Dorset sprinkled in. The quiet high street reflects tough economic times rather than a peaceful village but the town's setting by the River Avon redeems the neglected ambience and after a riverside walk among the willows and perhaps a run-around in the children's play area, you begin to appreciate this former market town. The Avon Valley Path passes through Fordingbridge.

It's well worth visiting the **Fordingbridge Museum** (*King's Yard, SP6 1AB; 01425 655222; www.fordingbridgemuseum.co.uk; open Easter– Oct*), especially for the small collection of paintings and sketches by Augustus John of his children. At one time considered Britain's leading portrait painter, John lived at Freyerns Court in Burgate, near Fordingbridge, for the last 31 years of his life until his death in 1961. A timeline at the front of the museum explains Fordingbridge's historical context and other items show how life has changed for town residents. The well-presented displays grew from the private collection of former town residents John Shering and his brother Richard, who amassed some 9,000 artefacts from house clearances and shop closings. A large Victorian doll's house donated by a local is meticulously furnished. Adjacent to the museum is a visitor information centre.

At the opposite end of the high street, **Branksome China** is known to a small but discerning clientele for its distinctive lily bowls on pads and classic two-toned tableware that undergoes a 24-hour firing process. The beautiful pieces created in this unassuming factory are surprisingly little known; a look in here is highly recommended.

An eccentric and delightful Fordingbridge tradition is the carpet of flowers which appears each year at **St Mary's Church** in Church Street. The themed display, which curves along the aisles and around pillars beneath the soaring arches, is well worth a visit. It's usually held on a weekend in June, but there is no specific date.

Food and drink

Bridges 26 High St ① 01425 654149. This small tea room at the centre of the high street is a pleasant spot for breakfast and lunch or a slice of cake in the afternoon.

The George 14 Bridge St ① 01425 652040 ⑩ www.georgeat fordingbridge.co.uk. This has the prime location for viewing the Avon and its resident swans that swim right past your table. In summer, the few tables on the outdoor terrace are in high demand but you still get a good view inside from the conservatory or the large back room with a fireplace. The interior is cosy and welcoming although service can be slow during busy times, and they serve the best pub food in town.

⑥ Woodgreen Village Hall

Woodgreen, near Fordingbridge SP6 2AQ ☎ 01725 513828
Ⓦ www.woodgreenvillagehall.org.uk. Phone to see the interior, or visit
during a public event.

The sleepy exterior of Woodgreen belies the community spirit beneath.
Not only did villagers unite to save their community shop, but they
are fiercely proud of their village hall. Life in the 1930s is depicted in
a series of Grade II listed **wall murals** painted by two Royal College
of Art students who were paid £100 to live in the village while they
worked on it. Exercising their mutual passion for early Italian frescoes,
each artist painted one side and one end wall. One of them, Robert
Baker, who went on to become an Oxford professor, loved Woodgreen
so much that he retired here; he is buried in the village cemetery.

Every inch of wall is painted with scenes of village life, including
a flower show, cider pressing, a Sunday school gathering and a dance
contest. 'It's amazing how many of these things we still do,' said Margaret
Wendell, the town hall caretaker, who told me the horticultural show
depicted on the wall is still held here every other year.

Residents of the village, some of whom are still alive today, were models
for the paintings. Only one person appears twice. The local poacher,
who is shown with his gun in a scene illustrating the River Avon from
Castle Hill, returns to the village on the opposite wall as a respectable
citizen playing his accordion. Flanking the stage are representations of
the morning cock crowing and an owl hailing darkness.

Perhaps the most wonderful aspect of the murals is that they are not
tucked away for safekeeping. The village hall is still a central point in
village life and hosts regular meetings, displays and a playschool group.
Outside the window, three black cherry trees, known locally as 'Merry
trees', have been planted. As Margaret and I surveyed them she laughed
and explained that they are depicted in the artwork because villagers
used to concoct a drink from the cherries that made them merry.

If you want to see this representation of bucolic village life, and I
recommend that you do, you can arrange an appointment with
Margaret (at the number given above), who remembers some of the
people portrayed in the scenes. 'I always think I've seen every detail but
every once in a while I'll notice something I didn't before,' she told me
as we admired the walls. 'I feel protective of this art. This is our history.'
Margaret has lived in the village for 47 years and held her wedding
reception in the hall.

Woodgreen Community Shop

Hale Rd, SP6 2AJ ℡ 01725 512467 🌐 www.woodgreencommunityshop.org.

'This is the pride of our village,' said Andrea Finn, gesturing to the shelves neatly stocked with baked goods, jams, herbs, chutneys and sauces, all made and grown by residents of Woodgreen and other nearby villages. Further back, fridges containing local meats and cheeses and shelves with wines and household goods awaited the day's customers. We sat at a table by the large window that overlooks the lane and fields beyond. The post office window was open and a new day began at the Woodgreen Community Shop.

As people came in and waved to Andrea, it was hard to believe that this shop, like so many others nationwide, was threatened with closure in 2006. 'When the couple who ran the previous shop and post office had to give it up due to ill health, Sue Alpress and I placed a notice in the parish newsletter urging people to get involved and try to save it.' Responses were enthusiastic and in just six weeks, concerned citizens from Woodgreen and the nearby villages of Breamore, Godshill and Hale, all of which had lost their shops, raised over £16,000 in shares and donations. In January 2007 the Woodgreen Community Shop Association took over the running of the village shop and post office. And that was just the beginning.

The Association went on to build a new £350,000 building that is more than double the size of the original quarters. 'The committee of eight and a large number of volunteers brought a diverse range of skills that enabled us to pull it all together, but there was a steep learning curve,' explained Andrea, whose background is in organising art shows. 'It was a long five years of research, community consultation, finding land, appointing architects, securing planning permission, and everything else associated with building a new, sustainable premises. In addition there was writing a business plan, applying for grants and organising fundraising activities.' About a third of the money was raised from community events; the sales of £10 shares (there are now over 500 shareholders); and donations. The remainder came from grants from a variety of organisations.

Meanwhile, the committee formed of locals established a Product Development Group to research farmers and producers in the New Forest, Wiltshire and Dorset. 'We try to stock as locally as possible including New Forest Marque items and if that's not possible then we look to regional producers.'

Now that things are up and running, volunteers are still essential. 'Paid staffers run the post office and shop, but there are lots of shelves to be stacked, boxes to unload and rubbish to be cleared,' said Andrea. 'It's been challenging for the committee to change from the objective of planning and building to the daily running of the shop.' As I chatted with Andrea and volunteers, I was impressed by the dedication and pride of this group who have not just brought a shop to the village but engendered a sense of community that recalls a simpler age. Some 40 volunteers work at Woodgreen.

'The shop, even in its planning stages, has pulled the community together. It's a great way for newcomers to meet people and for people who have left work to continue to have a worthwhile job.' Even though Andrea is frequently the main spokesperson, she insists: 'It's not my shop. It's all of ours – the entire community has been involved from the outset and has a real sense of ownership'.

Andrea has discovered that the shop's coffee maker and indoor and outdoor tables are popular with walkers and cyclists. The shop is an official New Forest Information Point where staff answer questions about the Forest and direct tourists to where they can get help finding accommodation. There is even a tethering point and water bowl for dogs outside the door. As I left, several villagers had gathered by the fresh bread display to catch up on local news. 'Despite the incredibly hard work, it's been worth doing,' Andrea said, with a broad smile.

North and west borders: weaving in and out of the New Forest

You can feel the presence of Wiltshire as you head to the **northern reaches**, possibly because the views of patchwork fields are such a marked contrast to the woodland and heaths of the Forest. Whatever the difference, the relative quiet and absence of tourist attractions is a striking change from the busy southern Forest.

It's fun to weave in and out of Hampshire, Dorset, Wiltshire and back again. The wonderfully unspoilt landscapes of **Martin Down** and **Cranborne Chase** are worth further exploration; this is a taster. The gentle slopes of wide-open grass in Martin Down Nature Reserve has its own distinctive qualities both aesthetically and in terms of wildlife.

⑦ Downton

Downton, originally within the borders of William the Conqueror's New Forest, has been populated for over 7,000 years, making it one of the oldest settlements in the area. The **Downton Heritage Trail**, which is available at the post office as a leaflet or a more detailed guide, is an absorbing delve into the best of the area outlining some of its varied history. The trail begins at the 13th-century **cross** at the heart of the Borough, the most eye-catching part of town with its long, narrow green lined with thatched houses. From there, the trail continues out to the

Welcoming spring with the Cuckoo Fair

Historians believe that Downton hosted market fairs from 1249 but the first proper cuckoo fair was probably held in 1530. Cuckoo fairs evolved to celebrate the arrival of warm weather, so named because the cuckoo is a migratory bird that returns in spring.

World War I brought an end to most village fairs and Downton was no exception. But in 1980, Steve Addison, a newcomer to the area, led a group of volunteers in re-establishing the fair. It's been running ever since, as an annual, non-profit event held on the Saturday of the first bank holiday weekend of May. Its growth to the huge occasion that it is today, with some 20,000 people attending, is testimony to what volunteers can achieve.

Stalls line the green strip of The Borough, one of Downton's most attractive streets with its profuse showing of thatched roofs. Crafts, jewellery, woodcarvings, paintings and lots of home-baked goods are on offer. An empty car park is dedicated to food producers, which include local butchers, jam- and honey-makers, bakers and wineries. Some of the exhibitors display the New Forest Marque (see page xix).

There is, of course, a maypole around which local schoolgirls dance throughout the day. If you arrive at the start, you can witness the crowning of the princess and the procession from the Bull Hotel to the maypole that officially opens the event.

In keeping with the ancient tradition of minstrels and performers who would come to the village during the fair, there are lots of local bands and entertainers as well as a field with fairground rides and games. It's a great, old-fashioned day out and well worth a special trip – as long as you don't mind hordes of people.

water meadows where you still can still see the old sluice gates which were controlled by 'drowners' to flood the meadows and encourage early grazing. A visit to the **old mills and tannery** are a reminder of the importance of the River Avon in this village's industrial history.

The Moot

The Heritage Trail passes **The Moot**, an 18th-century garden created from the site of a Norman castle built by the bishop of Winchester. These peaceful and unusual eight acres abut the banks of the River Avon.

Various shops in town should have a leaflet to self-guide you but the library is probably the most likely to have it in stock. The gardens are just a short distance from the library, go up the high street and then turn right into Moot Lane where the entrance is on the right, opposite **Moot House**. There is a car park just beyond.

You have to use a lot of imagination to figure out what might have been here in the 12th century, but the gardens are delightful to walk through. The original earth structure was built by the Bishop of Winchester, brother of King Stephen, to control the crossing of the River Avon and was destroyed after the bishop's death in 1154.

In 1700, when Moot House was built, the earthworks were landscaped as a garden. The best surviving feature of this time is the **amphitheatre**, made up of six tiers of grass which overlook a small pond. Drama productions are still staged here as well as in the **Sunken Garden**.

In 1972, the gardens were separated from Moot House, at which time they became overgrown. In 1988, local residents formed a charitable trust to restore them to the way they were in 1909. The site is maintained largely by volunteers who will happily guide private groups (*www.downton.org.uk/moot_home.htm*).

You can very clearly see the inner and outer ditches. The area between the two was used for livestock and people lived here when an invasion was feared. The two mounds in the centre are the remains of the castle keep. Climb up **Bevis Mount** (it's steep and not suitable for everyone) for a far-reaching view of Wiltshire hillsides toward Cranborne Chase and Clearbury Rings, an Iron Age hillfort.

⑧ Breamore

Life in this bucolic spot seems to be continuing on seamlessly from the 16th century, when the original Breamore House was built. The village's history stretches back to Saxon times, when the church of St Mary was founded, and beyond. In the Roman period, the land most likely was part of the estate at the Roman Villa at Rockbourne.

Breamore House and Countryside Museum

℗ 01725 512858 ⓦ www.breamorehouse.com. Open Apr–Oct.

You can get a genuine feel for life in the 19th century by visiting the **Countryside Museum** just inside the gates of the estate. The life-size shops and farmworker's cottage illustrate how villages were once self-sufficient. Each person in the community was dependent on the others and in this way the village survived daily life.

An impressive collection of horse-drawn and steam-operated farming equipment fills the barns. Although these are interesting enough in themselves, they impressively come to life during the museum's **working weekends** in the spring and autumn. You might get to see the grinding mill churning away or the Dreadnought, a 1926 haulage tractor which takes two-and-a-half hours just to get started. It certainly gives you the impression that some people back then worked hard. Just a quick glance at the village laundry is enough to convince you that today's domestic chores aren't really so bad.

A short walk up the elegant drive takes you to **Breamore House**, which you can visit only on a scheduled tour. Although the exterior is the way the house would have looked when it was built in 1583, the original interior was destroyed in 1856. When I first visited it, I thought that my guide, an elderly gentleman looking rather dapper in his tie and jacket, knew an extraordinary amount about all the paintings and antiques in this country house. When someone in my group inquired about the six children who presently live here, his face lit up as only a grandfather's could and I realised that our guide was Sir Edward Hulse, 10th baronet of Breamore. Apparently when the scheduled guide called in sick, Sir Edward just took his turn at showing visitors around his home. Although it might test your patience to have visitors tramping through your house and gardens throughout the summer, Sir Edward was as congenial and welcoming as if we were friends whom he'd invited around for afternoon tea.

Breamore House exudes charm even without the owner as host. Despite its grand exterior, the house feels intimate and it's easy to imagine children racing up and down the staircase or elegant ladies taking tea in the drawing room.

The Hulse family purchased the property in 1748 and the house contains some of the art and furniture they have accumulated over the last 250 years. The most important collection, Sir Edward explained proudly, is the 14 paintings by a son of Murillo that show the intermingling of various Indian races. They hang in an alcove above the main staircase and are the earliest known set of ethnological paintings.

While there, I also spotted a Rembrandt, four Van Dycks and a large rural scene by David Tenniers which hangs in the Great Hall. The two 17th-century Brussels tapestries are in excellent condition and help soften this otherwise rather long room. Look out for the portrait of Christian Dodington, widow of William Dodington, who owned the house and committed suicide in 1600. When the Hulse family purchased the house, it was with the agreement that the portrait would not be moved, and so it still hangs above a door in the Great Hall. This rectangular room has its own special history: during the planning of the D-day invasions, General George Patton headquartered here for a short time while allied troops waited and camped in the nearby New Forest.

The kitchen is warm and inviting and has an abundance of copper pans and kettles arrayed on shelves. 'The Hulse family had only sons,' explained Sir Edward, 'so the copper stayed here with the girls.'

Church of St Mary

Just at the base of the drive leading to the house is the church of St Mary, built roughly around AD1000 and one of the finest surviving Saxon buildings in southern England. It has an **unusually long nave** and the walls are made of whole flints with large quoins of irregular long and short work (a characteristic feature of Saxon church building) and pilaster strips of green sandstone and ironstone. The original stones on the northeast quoin of the chancel are still visible. Another remarkably well-preserved feature is the strikingly clear **Anglo-Saxon inscription** above the door from the tower through to the south porticus, believed to mean 'Here is manifested the word to thee.' Seven of the original **Saxon windows** remain: two can be seen high in the wall on the north side of the nave and another in the south transept. Others have been altered. Although it is not technically a cruciform church, St Mary's represents an evolutionary step in the cruciform plan due to its integration of tower and transepts of the same width all connected as one structure.

Before the 12th century, the church was a minster, serving the needs of surrounding communities. The original church was larger and is thought to have been part of a royal estate, but in the 15th century parts of the building that had fallen into disrepair were destroyed. By then the community did not need such a large church because the population had declined due to the Black Death, and there was insufficent money for repairs.

Food and drink

Bat and Ball Inn Salisbury Rd, SP6 2EA ℗ 01725 512 252. Average pub fare in a pleasant setting with a large garden and children's play area. Staff are friendly and the location is convenient, on the A338, less than a mile from Breamore House.

The Tea Barn Breamore SP6 2DF ℗ 01725 512858 ⓦ www.breamore house.com. Situated in the courtyard of the Countryside Museum, this small café which serves light lunches and cream teas is open the same hours as the house and museum (though sometimes opens 11.30am) but can be visited separately. Best when you can sit outside.

A walk to the mysterious Breamore Mizmaze

You can walk to **Breamore Mizmaze** from Breamore House. About a mile through the woods, this is one of only eight surviving turf labyrinths in England. The Mizmaze, technically a labyrinth because it has no junctions or crossings, is fenced for protection but you still experience a mystical sensation with the encircling yew trees and atmosphere of secrecy. In the nearby woods you can see temporary shelters built from logs and ground cover – a sure sign that this site is still used for sacred pilgrimages. It is thought that in its early days, the mizmaze was used by monks from Breamore Priory who absolved their sins by crossing the turf on their knees, saying prayers at specific points. Whether or not their sins were forgiven, this would have kept the chalky paths visible. Now, there are tales of modern-day fertility ceremonies and spooky encounters with apparitions, but I've been there several times on my own and have only encountered peace and quiet.

This route incorporates the site of Whitsbury Castle as well as Breamore church and Breamore House. There also are some beautiful views of farmland and thatched cottages around a green at Upper Street. The five-mile course is simple to follow and, aside from a few gentle hills and potentially muddy ground on the bridlepaths, easy to walk. You could instead start from Breamore House.

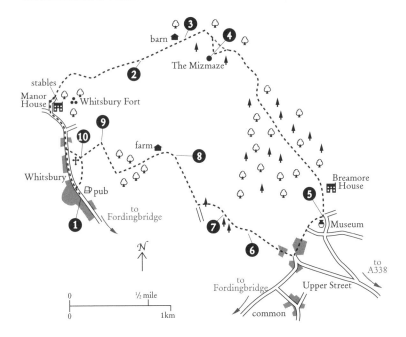

Begin in Whitsbury, four miles northwest of Fordingbridge. There are a few parking spaces opposite the Cartwheel Inn and a few more up the road by the letterbox in the village. Grid reference SU128189.

❶ With the Cartwheel Inn on your right, walk up the main street of Whitsbury for about half a mile. Go past the sign on the right to Whitsbury Manor Stud and the church, and where the road curves left follow the surfaced track on the right, marked 'Bridleway' (not the sharp right to Manor House). Continue for about 50 yards, then veer right behind the stables and on to the bridleway with woods on the right. If you look carefully into this fenced, overgrown area, you can see the ramparts and ditches of **Whitsbury Castle**, the 16-acre site of an Iron Age hillfort. Continue on the path downhill for half a mile.

❷ At the bottom of the hill, cross the track and go over the style ahead that is slightly to the right and might be hidden in undergrowth. Follow the grassy track uphill between two fields before it enters woods and then continue forward, ignoring the cross-tracks.

❸ The track soon emerges into the open, following the right edge of a field to the gate by the next group of trees. Beyond the gate, turn right, then shortly bear right towards the wood, following the vague imprint of a track. Walk along the edge of the wood until you see a sign (the back will be facing you) to **Breamore Mizmaze**.

❹ After visiting the Mizmaze, return to the track which soon bends left and runs between hedges. Shortly, the track enters woods; avoid side turns and proceed all the way to the bottom, emerging into the grounds of **Breamore House**, which is on your left.

❺ Follow the driveway down to the gateposts with stone lions and turn right towards the **Countryside Museum**. Turn left through the tea shop grounds and walk straight through to the drive with the picnic area on your right. Turn right on to the road and walk through the hamlet of Upper Street. Take the next right at the grassy triangle on to Rookery Lane.

❻ Where the road ends, walk straight ahead on to the track that runs between hedges and is marked with a yellow arrow, not the left-hand track marked with a blue arrow.

❼ Follow this narrow path for about 250 yards where it forks right and reaches a gate, then continue forward along the left side of a field to pass through another gate and turn right on to a track.

❽ After a quarter of a mile, just as the track begins to bend right, follow the track on the left leading to a farm. Pass straight through the farmyard (the gate at the entrance is heavy) and pick up a track at the far end marked by a line of trees on the right-hand side. The track leads up to woods, at the far side of which you turn right.

❾ Walk with paddocks on your left and you will see **Whitsbury church** on the other side. Where the track meets the end of a surfaced road by a bungalow on the right, turn left and walk straight on the track between fences towards the church, which is now hidden among the trees. Turn left at the T-junction of tracks and walk around the bend where you can enter the churchyard through the gate on the right.

❿ In front of the church, with Whitsbury in view below, either take the gate and proceed down to another gate by a thatched building to emerge close to the pub or if you parked further up in the village, go through the gate at the far end of the churchyard, opposite the church entrance, which leads on to a narrow, fenced path through the woods and down to the village.

⑨ Rockbourne

One of the most photogenic villages in Hampshire, Rockbourne is laid out in a linear pattern typical of the area. There is no central focus, with thatched houses lining the meandering main street. It makes a pleasant amble, combined with lunch at the Rose & Thistle; you can park in the village hall car park.

Rockbourne Roman Villa

℗ 01725 518541 ⓦ www3.hants.gov.uk/rockbourne-roman-villa.
Open Apr–Sep.

Who would believe that a ferret could uncover Roman ruins? But that's what happened in 1942. A farmer who was digging out a ferret from a rabbit warren found an oyster shell and tile. Morley Hewitt, a local estate agent and antiquarian recognised the potential significance of these items and dug a trial hole which immediately uncovered a mosaic floor. He subsequently bought the land but because it was wartime, excavations didn't begin until 1956. Digging continued annually in the summer months but unfortunately, early excavators discarded some useful finds like animal bones and pottery shards. They also failed to record the exact archaeological contexts that might have shed light on how the Roman villa had been laid out.

Even so, experts have worked out how buildings might have been arranged and the villa, which would have contained about 40 rooms together with farm buildings at its peak in the 4th century, is now marked out in the field. There are explanatory plaques explaining the different areas and how the inhabitants might have lived when the villa was in use.

One highlight is the **hypocaust**, the foundation of the underfloor heating system, which heated the bathhouse. It is unusual here in comprising curved roof tiles cemented together to form the supporting *pilae* rather than a stack of flat bricks. You can also see portions of mosaic floors which have been restored and relaid. Archaeologists have determined that the first phase of building featured one simple rectangular house over the remains of an Iron Age timber roundhouse.

It's best to start inside the **museum** which explains how the remains were discovered and excavated. Display cases contain artefacts including coins, jewellery, hairpins, basic tools and a roof tile of Purbeck stone. In 1967, an undoubtedly delighted summer volunteer discovered a pottery jar filled with 7,717 bronze coins. They could have been buried to protect them from an outside threat or possibly as an offering to the gods. By examining coins, experts determined that the site was occupied for about 350 years. By the 5th century, the villa was abandoned and walls were demolished and quarried for stone.

Nature notes displayed alongside archaeological information add another dimension to the site. During school holidays, special activities are conducted for children designed to inspire them to see the ruins as more than a big field with a few stones laid out.

From the ruins you can see the somewhat incongruous tower of the **Eyre Coote Monument** which stands in the grounds of West Park. Its aesthetics are questionable but the 100-foot column is a great way to orient yourself when walking in the fields surrounding Rockbourne.

Food and drink

Rose & Thistle Rockbourne SP6 3NL ℗ 01725 518236
Ⓦ www.roseandthistle.co.uk. A 16th-century pub that has gone gastro without losing its charm. The low ceilings and huge fireplace make this a cosy place for lunch or dinner and the food, more restaurant than pub fare, is an added bonus. Book ahead as there are few tables. In summer the small front garden is a prime lunch or post-walk drinking spot.

⑩ Martin Down National Nature Reserve

This is prized as one of the best places in the country to observe a large variety of **butterfly** species. The southern section of the reserve is located near **Martin**, the most westerly settlement in Hampshire and a top contender for quintessential chocolate-box village.

Martin Down has two car parks: one on the A354, the road that runs between Salisbury and Blandford Forum and serves the northern part of the reserve and the other at the eastern edge of the reserve at Sillens Lane, just under a mile from the village of Martin. Regardless of which you use, the easiest way to get to both is from Martin. The car park on the A354 is reachable by driving northwest through Martin and then turning left on to the A354, heading west. The reserve's car park is after about a mile on the left.

You can explore varied habitats. Across the A354, is the northern part of the reserve, some 45 acres of scrubland and woodland that is carefully trimmed to provide optimum habitats for birds, butterflies, snakes and other woodland wildlife. I joined Robert Lloyd, Reserve Manager, on one of the occasional guided walks he gives around the reserve, usually in summer.

In the area called **Kitt's Grave**, woodland butterflies flourish: on a summer morning I counted ten different types, including white admiral, silver-washed fritillary, marble white and dark green fritillary. Between April and September a weekly census is taken to monitor butterfly populations. This land is not grazed and cutting is done on rotation during the winter so as not to disturb any nesting wildlife. 'This is where the staff work because the work on the Downs is all done by sheep,' joked Robert, referring to the grazed downs on the other side of the A354. 'It's not rocket science but if you get it wrong you will lose species. Because this is a nature reserve, we have the luxury of time and we can tinker with it to get it right for a variety of species.' A bit of folklore surrounds the legend of the grim name for this area but the most frequently heard story is that a gypsy called Kitt died on the boundary between two parishes, neither of which would pay for her burial. So she was buried where she was found and the copse was named after her.

Throughout this woodland are numerous reminders of the past. Near the main road the remains of a Roman road are visible just inside the entrance gate. After passing around the cattle grid, go through the first gate on the right into **Vernditch Chase**. Archaeologists believe that the mound on the left with the ditch running alongside it is a vestige of the Roman road. In spring and early summer you have a chance of seeing several species of rare orchid here, including bee and butterfly orchids but you need to look closely, as they grow very near to the ground.

In the woodlands is a **Neolithic long barrow**. At the entrance to Kitt's Grave, go straight on to the main trail. If you follow this around in a 'U' shape, the barrow, excavated in the late 19th century by Augustus Pitt Rivers, is on the left. Many of the recovered materials are in the Pitt Rivers Museum in Oxford.

On the other side of the A354, straight behind the car park, is a linear prehistoric earthwork, **Bokerley Dyke**, which runs near the former World War II firing range. Butterflies thrive in the sheltered environment. The downland here has been unploughed for centuries since the first farmers cleared the woodland in Neolithic times. The open spaces were grazed by animals and today Natural England keeps about 120 sheep here in summer and close to 800 in winter, supplied by local graziers, to keep the scrub at bay. The unploughed land allows many wildflowers to flourish in the ancient chalky soils where grasses cannot compete. In the middle of summer, the reserve is carpeted in purple scabious and knapweed.

If you park at **Sillens Lane** on the eastern side of the reserve, you can walk up the hill to the ridge for a view of the New Forest on one side and Hampshire and Wiltshire farms on the other. The gorse and tree growth at the top does not permit an unimpeded view but it's worth the climb. There are well-cleared tracks on the hillside but part of the pleasure here is that you can wander wherever you please and find yourself completely alone. If you are looking for butterflies, walk west from the car park keeping the hedgerow on your right and the field (flower-filled in spring and summer) on your left.

Food and drink

The Compasses Inn, Damerham ① 01725 518 231 ⓦ www.compassesinn damerham.co.uk. Dog biscuits at the bar are the first indication of the relaxed atmosphere at The Compasses. The bonus is that the kitchen produces well above-average pub food. The very spacious and well-landscaped garden makes a delightful lunch spot and the main dining room or bar is a cosy place to eat in the evening. There are always four real ales, including Ringwood's Best Bitter and often a local guest beer.

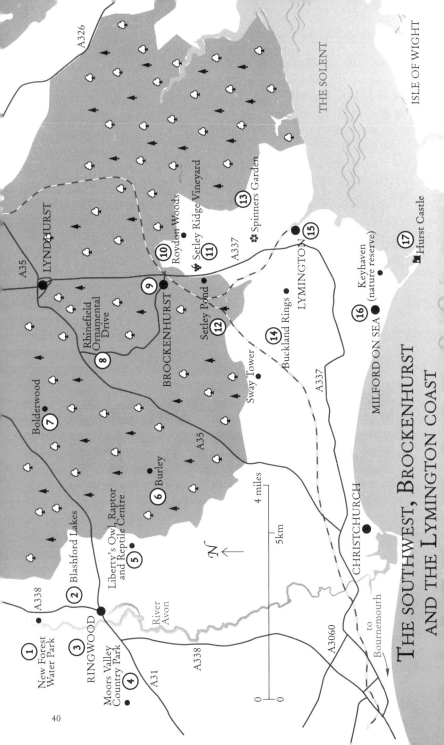

THE SOUTHWEST, BROCKENHURST
AND THE LYMINGTON COAST

ISLE OF WIGHT

THE SOLENT

A326

① New Forest Water Park

② Blashford Lakes

③ RINGWOOD

④ Moors Valley Country Park

A338

A31

River Avon

A338

A3060

to Bournemouth

CHRISTCHURCH

⑤ Liberty's Owl, Raptor and Reptile Centre

⑥ Burley

⑦ Bolderwood

⑧ Rhinefield Ornamental Drive

⑨ LYNDHURST

A35

BROCKENHURST

Sway Tower

A35

⑩ Roydon Woods

⑪ Setley Ridge Vineyard

⑫ Setley Pond

⑬ ❀ Spinners Garden

A337

Buckland Rings

⑭

LYMINGTON

⑮

A337

Keyhaven (nature reserve)

⑯ MILFORD ON SEA

⑰ ⌘ Hurst Castle

N

0 ——— 4 miles

0 ——— 5km

40

2
THE SOUTHWEST
BROCKENHURST AND THE
LYMINGTON COAST

The glories of this part of the
Forest are not along the main
roads. In the suburban and
somewhat rushed central
part and western edges of
the Forest, particularly
around Ringwood and the
A338, the area loses some
of its distinctive qualities.
But within seconds of
leaving major roads, you can be on a
quiet country lane or even deep within
Forest woodland.

Ringwood is a busy market town, made all the more so because of its
proximity to the A31 and natural affiliation with points further west.
For shopping, it's the most useful of all the villages and towns in and
around the New Forest; if you need something, you are most likely to
find it here.

Burley and **Brockenhurst** very much belong to the New Forest.
Animals roam freely throughout the streets, almost as if the towns
are afterthoughts and the Forest has surrendered a bit of land to
accommodate human residents' needs. The boundaries of both flow
seamlessly into Forest, especially in Burley where the main shopping
area is very tiny. It is a tourist haven, but the beauty of Burley is its
surrounding Forest. Leaving Burley to the north through Burley Street
and on to Vereley Hill offers gorgeous views and walking, as does the

Forest around South Oakley Inclosure (where there is a bike trail quickly reached from the village centre). Brockenhurst has a more suburban feel in the streets surrounding the village centre but its high street is pure village. It is my favourite of all Forest enclaves, a lovely place to potter around and have a coffee, often in the company of ponies and cows that regularly wander around.

Easy **cycling** is especially rewarding around the central Forest. The Forest network of cycle paths is centred around Brockenhurst, including a disused railway line that provides a wide, flat route. You have to cycle on minor roads for a short time to access it from the village but not for very far. The other problem, as with many New Forest cycle tracks, is that it doesn't go in a continuous loop and you need to double back. But this works well if you've rented cycles in Brockenhurst. There are also several cycle trails in the woods around the Rhinefield Ornamental Drive; you can get all the way to Lyndhurst on designated trails. The area around Ober Water and Puttles Bridge just as you enter the Forest at Rhinefield Road (before the Ornamental Drive) is especially gratifying.

From the very Forest flavour of Brockenhurst, it's a short distance to the coastal atmosphere of **Lymington** where it's all about boats and the Solent. The town overflows with visitors in summer, because there is so much to do, from crabbing by the quay, swimming in the saltwater pool, walking along the marshes at Keyhaven or taking a ferry to the Isle of Wight. The main roads through here are not that appealing; stick to the coast and especially **Keyhaven**. The **Solent Way** passes right through Lymington, so it's possible to walk about ten miles east or west towards Beaulieu or Milford on Sea respectively. The Forest is not far – **Beaulieu Heath** is an easy cycle ride away and **Setley Plain** is a good place to walk to for its expansive views and concentration of prehistoric barrows.

In summer, my family is frequently found among the strawberry vines of **Goodall's Pick Your Own**, conveniently situated across from the ferry port.

Accommodation

Aldridge Hill Campsite Rhinefield Rd, Brockenhurst SO42 7QD ① 01590 623152 ⓦ www.campingintheforest.co.uk. A simple, back-to-nature

Forestry Commission campsite in a particularly pretty setting, bordered by two streams and very convenient for many Forest trails. This is 2 miles from the centre of Brockenhurst and has 200 pitches; no electricity or facilities; you'll need your own chemical toilet. Open summer only.

Cottage Lodge Sway Rd, Brockenhurst SO42 7SH ⓣ 01590 622296 ⓦ www.cottagelodge.co.uk ⓔ enquiries@cottagelodge.co.uk. 'We've been recycling since 1650', laughed Christina, eco-conscious owner of Cottage Lodge in the centre of Brockenhurst. The main part of this 17th-century cottage was built from boat timber that was felled in the 12th century. Although the above-average price 16-room B&B is on a busy road, it's walking distance from the train station and the Forest so it's ideal if you are travelling without a car. Christina is working to 'bring the Forest inside' so three of the rooms are furnished with striking beds and tables hand-carved from Forest wood. Tables in the breakfast room are all made from one tree. Christina is all about responsible tourism and has won numerous awards for sustainability as well as for supporting local business. There is even a room where you can operate the television by pedalling a bicycle.

Long Meadow Campsite New Park, Brockenhurst SO42 7QH ⓣ 01590 622489 ⓦ www.longmeadowcaravans.co.uk ⓔ long.meadow@hotmail. com. Set well back from the A337 just behind New Park Manor, this private campsite is a large, flat field bordered on two sides by forest. It's likely to be quieter than larger campsites nearby because the 10.30pm quiet rule is strictly enforced. It's popular with families because of the easy access to the Forest with walking and cycling trails, and the many deer. You can walk to Brockenhurst through the woods or there is a bus stop on the main road outside the campsite. The simple shower and toilet facilities are clean, and many campers are repeat visitors, which might justify the slightly higher prices. There are 100 grass pitches and 11 electrical hook-ups which must be booked ahead. Note that even though this site is just beside the New Forest Showgrounds, it is closed during the Show. Open April–October.

The Mill at Gordleton Silver St, Gordleton SO41 6DJ ⓣ 01590 683073 ⓦ www.themillatgordleton.co.uk ⓔ info@themillatgordleton.co.uk. A true gem. Owner Liz Cottingham is an energetic ideas machine who constantly works to make the Mill better and better. From a stroll through the secret garden with its sculptures and art installations – including one that actually spans the stream – to a restful 'sit' to the backdrop of soothing waters, it's all Slow at this hotel with excellent food thrown in; there are few places in the Forest with outdoor dining as delightful as this. Its many green initiatives include a heat exchange unit that harnesses energy from the river for heating and hot water. The cottage garden supplies herbs and many vegetables for meals. Of its eight immaculate bedrooms, the prize one is the Millars Suite located where the original mill's wheel was. The duck theme throughout is in honour of Crispie, the hotel's mascot and all her relatives whom Liz takes considerable pains to save from foxes. More expensive than a B&B, but breakfast is included and it is good value considering the quality of the rooms. The packages that include dinner are especially cost-effective. Highly recommended.

The Pig Beaulieu Rd, Brockenhurst SO42 7QL ① 0845 0779494 ⓦ www.thepighotel.com. All the appeal of an old-fashioned country house party but with a modern twist. From the grand drive to the plush sofas in the bar, it's a pampering experience. This slightly expensive 'restaurant with rooms' is very popular with the London set and has a buzzy ambience. There are 12 rooms in the main house, four in the courtyard, and the converted stables has nine, each with a horsey theme.

Sopley Lake Yurt Camp Derritt Lane, Sopley BH25 7AZ ① 01425 462 522 ⓦ www.forestyurts.com ⓔ info@forestyurts.com. If you want something completely different, this is it. Four yurts direct from Mongolia are situated by a lake on a private farm in Sopley, a short distance away from the Forest but well worth it if you want a good tale to recount. The interiors are cosy and tastefully furnished with a woodstove for chilly nights. The best part is the open-air kitchens with small ranges and basins overlooking the lake. A highly recommended camping/self-catering compromise, each yurt even has a private toilet and hot shower. No electricity, but the gas lamps are more atmospheric anyway. The elephant yurt sleeps eight and is ideal for groups. This is not cheap camping; you pay for the novelty factor but it's great value for families.

Upper Kingston Farm Cottages Upper Kingston, Ringwood BH24 3BX ① 01425 474466 ⓦ www.upperkingstonfarmcottages.co.uk. A working farm offering average-priced self-catering accommodation only just over a mile from Ringwood. Five airy cottages in a former stable, three of which are large enough for a family, are arranged around a courtyard where you can barbecue and picnic. Air-source heat pumps provide heating and hot water. Guests are given a welcome breakfast from the local farm shop upon arrival and can arrange grocery delivery or order from the nearby Crow Farm Shop. A large laundry facility has a notice-board listing things to do in the area. Accommodation can be arranged for your horse or bike.

Vinegar Hill B&B Vinegar Hill, Milford on Sea SO41 0RZ ☎ 01590 642979 ⓦ www.vinegarhillpottery.co.uk ⓔ info@vinegarhillpottery.co.uk. Not too many B&Bs have a built-in pottery studio where you can enjoy a weekend course as well as explore the area (see box, page 86). There are two well-priced doubles, one with a separate sitting room and one at the top of winding outdoor stairs. The prize accommodation (summer only) is Rosie, a refurbished caravan with a cosy double bed. Hot breakfasts, including eggs from the family hens and award-winning sausages from the village butcher, are delivered to rooms.

Wilf's Cabin, Burley BH24 4HT ☎ 01425 403735 ⓦ www.burleyrails cottage.co.uk ⓔ stay@burleyrails.co.uk. This simple self-catering log cabin deep in the Forest near Burley provides the rare opportunity to lodge within an ancient New Forest inclosure. Owner Ian Thew runs the New Forest Shooting and Fishing School and his wife Tracy is also a qualified fly-fishing coach. You can board your horse in the stables and have use of a paddock. Eggs from roaming chickens and home-baked bread are available and Tracy will cook meals upon request. It's expensive but a one-of-a-kind location. Well-behaved dogs welcome for a small a extra charge. Highly recommended. Good value if you bring horses.

Ringwood and Burley

Busy **Ringwood** ranks as the most useful of all the villages and towns in and around the New Forest for shopping and other town amenities, and offers easy access to the heart of the Forest and the beaches around Christchurch. The **River Avon** and its water meadows add a different dimension to this part of the Forest with fishing and abundant aquatic wildlife-viewing. At **Blashford Lakes** are excellent nature programmes for children, including pond dipping and mini-beast tracking; the bird hides give opportunities for observing a host of duck species. Further north on the A338, the focus is more on play at **New Forest Water Park** which offers waterskiing, wakeboarding, kayaking and paddleboarding with tuition for all ages. **Burley** offers carriage rides and deer safaris, while the holiday-camp atmosphere of **Moors Valley Country Park** is a contrast to the New Forest, with structured activities and instruction that can be a lot of fun for families.

① New Forest Water Park

Ringwood Rd, near Ringwood SP6 2EY ℗ 01425 656868 ⓦ www.newforest waterpark.co.uk. Open Easter–Oct.

You can hear the squeals of exhilarated children as you drive on the long, winding approach to the clubhouse that overlooks the two small lakes between Ringwood and Fordingbridge. Watersports include kayaking, wakeboarding, waterskiing, paddleboarding, and rides on inflatable bananas and Ringo tyres. Beach towels are flung across railings, balls whiz through the air while children await their turn boating and there is a true summer camp atmosphere. There are a range of packages incorporating both water fun and land-based sports including archery and football. Groups can hire the clubhouse where there are barbecues and buffets. Phone ahead to reserve a slot for a speedboat time. Unlike much of the Forest proper, you can have a camp fire here.

② Blashford Lakes

Ellingham Drove BH24 3PJ ℗ 01425 472760 ⓦ www.hwt.org.uk.

The nature reserve at Blashford Lakes, just outside Ringwood, shows what use can be made of abandoned gravel pits. Administered by the Hampshire & Isle of Wight Wildlife Trust (HIWWT), the Blashford Lakes Project runs many programmes.

Family events offered throughout the year aim to raise children's awareness of the wildlife that surrounds them. I attended a session here in which children gathered to observe evening wildlife. Michelle, an Education Officer with HIWWT, showed us a variety of animal skulls, deer antlers and plaster impressions of animal footprints. When she presented her samples of 'poo' and explained to children how to examine it for clues to animals' lifestyles, there were no cries of 'Eeew, gross,' but instead rapt concentration. Michelle then helped the children each make a humane trap which they later hid in the undergrowth in hopes of catching a mouse for observation. The children returned the next morning to find their traps and release the mice that had spent a cosy night in the box with food and hay.

At dusk, we walked out to one of the bird hides in the woods to observe wildlife. The children were thrilled to spot rabbits, a pheasant strutting his bright red colours and lots of small woodland birds. The *pièce de résistance* though was the bat monitors, small hand-held devices that bleep when bats are nearby. The success of spotting them seemed incidental to the excitement of working the monitor and being in the woods at nightfall.

③ Ringwood

Ringwood is a western gateway to the Forest and is a good shopping town. Residents often choose to live here because of its proximity to Dorset beaches and the Forest. It has its share of congestion; traffic on the A31, the major thoroughfare between Dorset and the New Forest (and ultimately London), inevitably slows down just before the Ringwood exit, especially on Friday and Sunday nights as people travel to and fro from country weekends.

The meandering **high street** has a somewhat uninspiring plethora of estate agents, banks, charity shops and the like, along with an assortment of bakeries and coffee shops, although some of the buildings in which they are housed have an old-world character. The best day to visit is Wednesday, when **Market Place**, which has been hosting a market since 1226, still has a pleasant bustle. The market itself has shrunk in recent years and nowadays traders sell clothing, shoes, crafts, plants, second-hand toys and food.

For people who lived here before 1989, the **Furlong shopping centre** development is tainted by the fact that this was the site of the town's long-running cattle market. It is a natural by-product of changing times but here in the Forest, all the more poignant as a bittersweet symbol of changing Forest ways.

The western end of town where the River Avon crosses, is the most pleasant, except for the relentless roar of the A31. Still there are a few walks along the river from here, most notably the **Avon Valley Path** which you can follow north for seven miles to Fordingbridge, passing through the Forest at Rockford and on to the water meadows outside Fordingbridge or south to Sopley, similarly passing through water meadows and a bit of woods.

Ringwood Meeting House

Meeting House Lane, BN24 1EY ① 01425 476188 Ⓦ www.ringwoodmeeting house.org

For an offbeat coffee break (mornings only) head to the Ringwood Meeting House, an extremely fine example of an early 18th-century

Ringwood's carnival

Residents put a lot of effort into the annual carnival, held in September. The all-day event features local marching bands, entertainers, a lengthy afternoon procession and a smattering of famous heavy horses. It's good old-fashioned, small-town fun for a place that, on the surface anyway, might be struggling to find its identity.

Presbyterian meeting house, just by the main car parks and bus stops. The nominal admission charge includes a cup of tea or coffee and a visit to the history exhibits, which line the walls and balcony. It no longer has a religious function but is obviously well cared for by the charity that now looks after it. Local theatre groups and musicians often perform here.

Tables have been set inside the remarkably well-preserved set of box pews so you can sip a cup of tea from the small kitchen area staffed by volunteers and imagine what it might have been like to be a non-conformist worshiper in the 1700s. Wealthy Ringwood residents purchased their box pews and willed them on when they died.

Ringwood Brewery

Christchurch Rd, BH24 3AP ☏ 01425 470303 ⓦ www.ringwoodbrewery. co.uk.

According to my guide, John, beer has been an integral part of Ringwood's development – since medieval man mixed River Avon waters with the malted barley of Hampshire. We gathered in the small on-site pub where we began the brewery tour with a sample. 'There will be plenty more afterwards,' John assured us. He related Ringwood's history as we sipped our half-pints. As a prominent market town, Ringwood required plenty of hostelries and pubs to refresh early salesmen who travelled here with their goods. There were as many as four breweries in Ringwood at one time but all had closed by 1925.

When CAMRA (the Campaign for Real Ale) was formed in the 1970s to encourage development of good quality cask ales, Ringwood local Peter Austin founded the brewery in a former bakery in an old Ringwood railway yard. He began brewing Best Bitter, still Ringwood's best seller. By the mid-1980s he was producing more varieties, had acquired a partner and had moved into larger premises that fittingly once had been a brewery. Austin became a leader in Britain's craft brewery market. Ringwood and surrounding towns are proud of their local brew but some may be disappointed when they realise the brewery is actually owned by the Midlands firm Marston's. Nevertheless, John told us that 'all is still run like a family business – it's surprising how much they leave us alone.'

There is not a huge amount going on as you tour the small factory except in the fermentation area where you can peer into giant tanks and watch and smell the yeast bubbling and brewing. 'Don't inhale too deeply, as the smell can be overpowering,' cautioned John. The concoction in the open tanks looks like a giant, toasted meringue with the occasional bubble at the surface as this molten mass works its way to your glass. John proudly informed us that the very first yeast culture from the brewery's beginnings is still at work and that there is a back-up sample locked away in Norwich in case anything goes wrong.

Back in the bar, we were offered unlimited refills – clearly this is a good value way to enjoy Ringwood Beer at its freshest. You can sample all four beers and you even get to take your glass home. Old Thumper, the flagship beer that won a CAMRA award in 1988, ultimately fostered the company's success. It has a complex flavour with caramel undertones that is deliciously distinct. My fellow tour members seemed intent on getting the most out of their ticket price.

The shop stocks t-shirts, bottled beers and mustards and sauces containing Ringwood brews. The marketing emblem of the Hampshire Hog was chosen because the hop flower isn't definitive enough, and indeed the friendly-looking statue in the car park seems an apt welcome to this light-hearted tour.

Food and drink

Frampton's High St, BH24 1BQ ① 01425 473114 ⑩ www.framptonsbar. co.uk. This eclectic café starts the day as a coffee shop serving pastries and cakes and transitions well to light lunches and then wine bar in the evening. Located in the building that once belonged to Frampton and Sons, a pet supply and garden shop that had been here for 175 years, the café has retained some original features, including shelving, floors and panelled walls. At the back is a sofa and some relaxing seating, while the front has communal tables. It all translates to a welcoming atmosphere.

The Castleman Trailway

From Ringwood you can cycle over 16 miles of former railway trackbed, formerly the Southampton to Dorchester line, by taking the Castleman Trailway into Dorset, through West Moors, Ferndown Forest and with a final section along the River Stour before ending in Poole.

④ Moors Valley Country Park

Despite its somewhat theme park atmosphere, Moors Valley earns a place in a Slow itinerary because of its excellent programmes that foster family togetherness while simultaneously teaching about the countryside. The structured activities are a good contrast to the wild setting of the New Forest and might give confidence to those who find the open Forest intimidating. The park gets very busy when school is not in session but even on crowded days you can find a corner for yourself. Technically, you could stay all day for just the price of parking but it's worth spending extra for some of the guided activities inside the park.

Deciduous woodland, coniferous forest, lakes, ponds and rivers make up the 250 acres of the country park. Activity trails for all ages are set up throughout the woods: there is one for exercise buffs, cyclists, walkers and those who want just to play. Nearly all the tracks are pushchair- and wheelchair-friendly. The adventure play area for older children is particularly good with a zip slide and lots of climbing challenges. It's possible to hire cycles, join a Go Ape programme for both juniors and adults, golf, fish and use the permanent orienteering course that caters to all ages and abilities. Children also love the steam train (it's kid-sized) which takes 20 minutes to run the mile-long track. If that doesn't keep you busy, explore the Forest on a hired Segway.

Fishing courses are fun and instructive here, particularly those for parents and children. Equipment is provided for those taking courses only. You don't have to take a course to fish but securing a swim (the specific places where you fish from; at Moors Valley they are mostly small gravel inlets) can be as competitive as getting a chair by the pool in a European resort. Some people come at 08.00 when the car park opens to claim their swim and then purchase a day ticket when the visitor centre opens at 09.00. All fishermen must have a rod licence from the Environment Agency.

For me, the most eye-opening feature at Moors Valley is the **orienteering**. The permanent course was mapped out by Wimborne Orienteering Club and you can challenge yourself with maps from the visitor centre, which offers courses for different levels. If you've never done orienteering, the introductory courses that run on the second Saturday of most months are excellent. 'Most visitors to the New Forest don't venture more than 30 yards from their car,' John Warren, my instructor and a member of Wimborne Orienteers told me. 'They are uncomfortable in the Forest.' I had signed up for an introductory session, not because I'm afraid of the Forest but because I have a very poor sense of direction and I wanted to become more comfortable reading maps. In a brief session, John taught me how to orientate myself with a map, study the key, read a compass and estimate distance. By the end, I felt more confident following a map in dense woodland.

Picnic tables at various places in the forest make a pleasant alternative to the small café. By the lake you can even bring a barbecue (provide your own rubbish bag).

⑤ Liberty's Owl, Raptor and Reptile Centre

Crow Lane, Ringwood, BH24 3EA ℡ 01425 476487 Ⓦ www.libertyscentre. co.uk. Open daily Mar–Oct and weekends Nov–Feb.

'Reptiles do not make good pets,' said Lynda Bridges firmly as she gazed at the enormous boa constrictor which she originally took in as an underfed, abused snake. 'People buy them as pets and then realise reptiles basically only eat and sleep so they neglect or abandon them.' Most of the reptiles at Liberty's are rescued, like the now healthy and seemingly happy constrictor.

When Lynda first took over the former New Forest Owl Sanctuary, people deposited terrapins, snakes and turtles on her doorstep and although she tried to house them, she doesn't have space to keep as many as she'd like. 'Perhaps it's because I have a farming background, I don't know, but I like animals and want to see them properly cared for,' she explained in a tour around the small reptile house. A common green iguana which Lynda adopted when the owner was surprised how large it had grown, gazed out at us from behind its glass shield and seemed to smile. 'There are now more reptiles than dogs in captivity,' Lynda lamented.

Because this is a relatively small wildlife centre, you'll get more out of your visit if you come for the daily flying displays of birds of prey.

These usually take place at noon and 15.00 but Lynda recommends phoning ahead to be sure. In summer there also is a reptile showing, usually at 14.00.

Lynda opened her menagerie, which she named after her prize Alaskan bald eagle, Liberty, in 2005 and is slowly revamping the rundown buildings that were part of the former owl sanctuary. She bought the site in 2003 when she heard that the entire facility was going to be razed and the animals put down. Linda's mission is an expensive and daunting one but the rescued owls don't seem to mind that some of the housing here is a bit tired and that renovations take time. 'I hope that when people come here they leave not only having learned about the animals that are here but about the importance of global conservation,' said Lynda. 'We need to make sure that children understand the need to care for animals so that their future is safe.'

⑥ Burley

Burley's claim to fame, which it's not shy about heralding, is its connection to **witchcraft**. Much of the hype centres on a white witch, Sybil Leek, who lived here in the 1950s and wrote several books on astrology and the occult. She founded **A Coven of Witches**, a shop selling broomsticks and spells for modern witches. Some people say that white witches still live in the Forest but none parade around with a jackdaw on their shoulder as did Sybil.

Most Burley residents consider the legend a concession to tourists who swarm this tiny village's streets in the summer months. Locals live a separate life. As one homeowner told me: 'Burley residents don't come out after 10.00 when the shops open. They come to town early to see friends and do errands and then they hurry away.' The centre is filled with ice cream parlours and shops flouting the witchcraft association; whether it's clever marketing or reality is left up to visitors to decide.

There is more folklore surrounding Burley. **Smugglers** who landed on the Solent coast, probably near Lymington and Beaulieu, escaped into the Forest and apparently used the **Queen's Head** pub as a stopping point. During renovations, workers found old coins, bottles and pistols hidden beneath floorboards.

Burley Wagon Rides

ⓣ 07786 371843 ⓦ www.wagonrides.co.uk. Rides are offered most days during school holidays and weekends.

It would be easy to dismiss Burley Wagon Rides as a tourist gimmick but there is an honourable tradition behind them. 'The wagon rides have been running from the Queen's Head car park for more than 30 years and Burley is the last village in the New Forest to offer them,' said Graham Mustey, current owner of the business. He and his partner, Karen, take people on long and short rides, 'depending on the mood of the group and how much people want to spend.' Most trips are a 20-minute ride through the Forest and on country lanes but Graham will do a longer journey through the inclosure if enough people are willing.

If you go on a ride, be sure to ask the very personable Graham about his horses. It's fascinating to hear about how to train horses to pull carts and work as a team. 'You begin by standing behind them and controlling the reins and then gradually introducing sound and weight so that they learn to cope with any situation.' Graham also uses his horses for ploughing, private hire for special occasions and for heavy horse musical shows. 'It's about keeping a tradition going.' In true Slow fashion, the schedule is not rigid so it's best to call ahead if you want to be guaranteed a place and to be sure they are operating.

New Forest Deer Safari

Ⓦ www.newforestsafari.co.uk. Safaris leave from the farm shop behind the Queen's Head Pub near the Burley public car park 12.00–17.00 every day in summer.

To a Forest resident, paying to ride out and view deer might be a laughable proposition. But that's what I found myself doing, all in the name of book research of course, with New Forest Deer Safari. Much to my surprise, it was enormous fun. I piled into a wagon with what seemed like an overwhelming number of young children and bounced along behind a tractor a couple of hundred yards or so over to Burley Park where a herd of red deer were obligingly waiting, knowing that the wagon contained goodies for them. As we jolted across the field, I could just make out very still antlers poking out from the long grass. Then gradually I could see more young red deer emerging from the woods as the tractor approached. When they realised we did indeed have food, they trotted towards the bucket and gave us a perfect view as they devoured the meal. The biggest treat was seeing an enormous stag with antlers so large that it seemed as if he would keel over on his head. He viewed the proceedings with interest but clearly it was beneath him to indulge in such easy pickings. As I watched two young males butt each other and grapple for food, I realised that the best views I normally have of deer in the Forest (aside from those who feast in my flower garden) are usually of their tail ends scampering away.

Food and drink

New Forest Cider (01425 403589; www.newforestcider.co.uk) produces dry, medium and sweet cider from local apples. Unless you are a cider fanatic, it's probably not worth a special trip but if you're in Burley, the small shop is interesting to peruse. Every autumn, this family-run business hosts an open weekend featuring traditional craft demonstrations and wagon rides from the village.

Survival therapy

Sunrise Bushcraft New Milton BH25 5AY ① 01425 618622 ⑩ www. sunrisebushcraft.com.

It's unlikely that you'd ever be stranded in the New Forest and need survival skills, even if you get temporarily misplaced, you are never far from a road. So it wasn't really necessary for me to enrol in a bushcraft survival course. But what I took away, in addition to some useful survival skills, was a deeper appreciation of how our ancestors might have lived in these woods. Now when I walk in remote parts of the Forest, I think about those who walked there before me, people who knew how to use every plant and animal and where to take cover, before the days of picnic lunches and designated car parks.

I joined James White, founder of Sunrise Bushcraft, in a private woodland just outside the Forest near Ringwood, for a one-day course in basic bushcraft survival. We began with fire-building skills – seven methods to be precise – all of which worked like a charm. I will never use newspaper to start a fire again. Now I know to find graded kindling, from skinny twigs to thicker branches, what James termed as 'ones, twos and threes'. By the end of the day, I could construct my own overnight accommodation from tree branches, leaves and compressed pine needles. I also learned that in the Forest what seems obvious isn't. I chose a lovely flat area beneath a beech tree to camp, figuring I'd be sheltered by the overhanging branches in case my structure wasn't rainproof. James then

Restaurants are not Burley's strong point. There is plenty of space but you won't have your most memorable meal here. The best bet is **The Cider Pantry** located in front of New Forest Cider, which serves tasty light meals and has a garden. **The Old Farmhouse Restaurant and Tea Rooms** has good food but it can be very slow at busy times. Otherwise, try the **White Buck Inn**, just to the east of town. Furnishings are tired but in summer the garden patio is pleasant.

Three Tuns Ringwood Rd, Bransgore BH23 8JH ① 01425 672232 ⓦ www.threetunsinn.com. Hanging baskets make this extremely popular thatched inn 3 miles southwest of Burley and just outside the national park look quite a picture in summer. Inside, the low-ceilinged main bar

informed me that beech trees drop limbs regularly and that I might not survive the night. Good to know.

We then walked through surrounding woods to identify edible and medicinal plants. With my penchant for the high-street chemist and local farm shop, I am unlikely to ever look for my medicines or dinner in the Forest, but touching, smelling and tasting woodland plants made me realise how distanced we humans have become from our environment. 'My goal isn't really to teach survival skills as much as it is to just get people out into the woods,' said James, who was born in the New Forest. 'People don't stop and live in the moment they rush from thing to thing – they don't even breathe properly. Sitting around the campfire, listening to owls, your heart rate drops and you start to breathe, really breathe.'

James's words hit home when he handed me a block of wood and a knife and suggested that I carve a tent peg. I was flummoxed. I barely knew what a tent peg was, let alone had the skills to make my own. I felt silly as I awkwardly attempted to make crude incisions. But gradually I got the hang of it and was lulled into a peaceful state in which my focus was solely on etching into the wood. The man perched on the log next to me hummed softly as he carved. 'Getting outside is important to maintain our sanity amid day-to-day stresses,' James told me later.

Sunrise, which works with young offenders, excluded children, and those with Asperger's and autism, also offers weekend courses which are popular with families. James is willing to help people find the suitable course for their needs and budget, and welcomes people to contact him.

is laden with old-fashioned character. The pub has been upping its game in the food stakes in the past few years. The atmosphere is lively so you won't have a quiet, romantic meal but the kitchen serves some of the best food in the area with refreshing takes on pub classics; seasonal menus mean interesting regular changes.

Brockenhurst and around

Brockenhurst is the ideal spot to base yourself in if you are travelling without a car. The Forest's main rail station and two bike rental shops are here along with many restaurants, cycle trails and places to stay that are within walking distance of the railway station. The village's population swells by thousands in the warmer months due to large campsites nearby and the annual **New Forest Show**, held here at the end of July. Some 95,000 people attend, so for three days the stretch of the A337, the Lyndhurst Road, between Lyndhurst and Brockenhurst is virtually impassable. It's best to avoid this area at opening and closing times, or go around via the A35.

Further south from Brockenhurst, **Setley Plain** is a mix of ancient barrows, mires and great expanses of heath that bloom cheerful yellow in summer and soothing purple in autumn. As brilliant as the colours are in sunshine, the brooding skies of cloudy days suit this landscape best when it's easy to imagine previous generations of horseriders galloping away to distant parts of the Forest.

⑦ Deer watching at Bolderwood

Bolderwood, a recreational area, is something of a Forest hotspot with its large car park, picnic area, deer sanctuary and flat green spaces at the edge of the woodland. In the **Information Unit** here, at weekends from Easter until September and daily during summer afternoons, you can speak to a volunteer ranger about deer, the royal hunting lodges that used to be on this land and ask general questions about the New Forest. The rangers have an excellent collection of antlers which you can touch. You'll have a good chance of seeing deer at the **observation platform** across the road from the car park. Although they have plenty to eat in the Forest, the keeper for this area, Andy Shore, feeds them in the meadow during the summer so that people have the opportunity to view them.

I joined an **evening deer watch**, a guided walk offered periodically throughout the summer by the Forestry Commission (*www.forestry .gov.uk*). I went reluctantly, as I view these antlered beasts as nothing but a nuisance in the garden, but I left with a more complete picture of Forest management, in particular the need for controlling the population of these destructive animals.

I also learned about the history of hunting and the royal hunting lodges that once graced this very site. 'You are walking in the footsteps of kings,' Derek, a volunteer ranger for the Forestry Commission, told us in his introduction to a brief history of royal hunting practices. The first record of a hunting lodge here is from 1325 but in 1358, when Edward III took over the Forest, he built four hunting lodges. The largest of these was at Bolderwood, then known as Hatheburgh and was situated where the picnic area is now. A series of lodges followed, the grandest of which was for the 1st Earl de la Warr, the Master Keeper in the early 18th century. Master Keepers viewed their role as a mark of distinction but the Under Keepers – 'who actually did the work,' according to Derek – were the ones who patrolled the Forest looking for poachers and wood thieves, and were the predecessors of today's Forest Keepers.

The fate of deer changed considerably as rulers came and went. The Normans took hunting so seriously that William I instilled Forest Law to protect the animals at the expense of Forest residents. Punishments were serious for those who interfered with the King's hunting ground. By the time of the Tudors, the Forest was viewed as a source of timber, so deer were perceived as pests that ruined trees, leading to widespread culling in the 17th century. James II, who ruled from 1685 to 1688, was the last monarch to hunt here. After that, timber interests really took over. By 1851, sentiments had come full circle and the Deer Removal Act authorised complete removal as they were a threat to the timber plantations and interfered with commoners' interests. A few fallow deer escaped the hunters and were able to bolster the numbers when demand for timber once again died down. Today, the population is carefully controlled by culling or else deer would destroy the Forest.

In the woods near the main car park, Derek showed us how to track the elusive animals. When they rub their antlers on trees, they leave gashes and will eventually cause the tree to die. Derek also pointed out that the greenery on all the trees was eaten below about head level of a deer. 'By observing the graze line and marks on the trees, you can determine when they are in the area.'

⑧ Rhinefield Ornamental Drive

This famous stretch of road is a bit less ornamental since the scourge of Sudden Oak Death, a disease that infects and kills oaks as well as numerous other New Forest species, including ash, beech, larch and conifers. Rhododendrons, which are not native to this area, can harbour spores of the fungus that can be transmitted to other species in rainwater. Several years ago, spores were found in rhododendrons on the ornamental drive so the Forestry Commission poisoned them in hopes of preserving the ancient Forest. Formerly you could drive along here and experience thrilling bouts of colour but now the ornamental

The work of a Forest keeper

Andy Shore looked up with a sheepish grin as he sprinkled feed on the ground by the observation platform at Bolderwood Deer Sanctuary. 'They don't need to be fed,' he explained, 'this is just to help visitors see them. Otherwise they prefer to hide in the Forest.' He called softly, knowing that the animals know him and trust him and that, sooner or later, they will appear. He pointed to a distant hill: 'There's one old woman up there, trying to decide whether to come down to the meadow. Should I or shouldn't I?'

I wouldn't even have noticed the lone female but to Andy, one of the Forestry Commission's keepers, she's like family. He knows many of the deer in his 'patch' as he calls it, around the Bolderwood area. Oddly, it's also his job to cull them when their numbers get too high but he doesn't feel sentimental about it; he views culling as essential to Forest maintenance and ultimately, preservation of the species themselves.

'The population would be unsustainable if we left them alone. We cull about 800 fallows each year and that just about maintains the population. This is not random culling but a very meticulous action plan based upon the needs of the Forest.' In April each year, a census is taken of the four main deer species in the Forest and from that a plan is designed for culling.

As a Forest keeper, a job that has been in existence since the 16th century, Andy is exercising ancient protection of 'vert and venison,' 'vert' being defined under the Forest law instituted by William the Conqueror, as 'everything that grows and bears a green leaf that may cover or hide a deer.'

drive is more about the grace and majesty of the tall conifers that were planted in the mid 19th century when it was fashionable to experiment with exotic trees. The road was originally the drive leading to **Rhinefield House**, a private home until the 1950s and now a hotel.

After Rhinefield House, the forest becomes thick with conifers. You can happily get lost amid towering trees that cast dark shadows or cool yourself down on a hot summer day. Midway along the drive is **Blackwater** car park. Of the many trails through the woods, a good one to do with children is the **Tall Trees Walk** which is a mile-long circular route between Blackwater and **Brock Hill** car parks. Plaques

'My job has changed little since those early days, except for maybe policing visitors.' Each of the Forest's eight keepers is responsible for a specific area, or beat. In addition to controlling the deer population, they are responsible for squirrels, hares and rabbits. They also liaise with the public and have the power to deal with civil offences, usually involving people camping in a non-official site or lighting a campfire.

Andy has been looking after the Bolderwood area for 25 years. Part of his job involves late night phone calls to attend to road accidents in which deer have been hit by a car or sometimes breaking up a late night party in the woods. More often than you think, Andy is summoned to pull a tourist from a bog deep in the Forest.

He describes his work with people with humour and perhaps a slight tinge of incredulity. 'People are only animals but highly predictable. I can tell who's going to be in the woods late at night just by the way their car is parked in the afternoon.'

As someone who has lived in the Forest his entire life and respects the ancient traditions, Andy is passionate about the Forest and his job. 'People forget that when it was established hundreds of years ago, the New Forest was given massive protection, even from the government. That protection is why we still have what we have today.'

He laments the loss of oral traditions that cease to be passed on as Forest life becomes diluted by outside forces. 'Not too long ago, 80% of the people living in the Forest also worked here. All that's changed as more people come from other areas and the Forest has become accessible to so many people. Society's detachment from nature means a loss of understanding for how the Forest works.'

along the trail highlight superlatives about the conifers including the forest's tallest tree and heaviest trees, Sequoias that are native to America. You'll also pass an inclosure bank and ditch which dates from 1848 and illustrates how foresters used to exclude animals from young trees without fencing. Benches throughout invite you to slow down and contemplate the magnificent heights that surround.

Also across from the Blackwater car park is the **Blackwater Arboretum**, a small area displaying trees from around the world. The wheelchair-accessible sensory trail encourages you to experience trees beyond the visual. On the other side of the very busy A35, the Rhinefield Ornamental Drive becomes the **Bolderwood Ornamental Drive** where just past the A35 you can see the famous **Knightwood Oak**, one of the oldest and most majestic trees in the Forest. The first car park on the left is Knightwood but the giant tree is actually across the road, among some newer ceremonial oaks. There are prettier trees in the Forest but the Knightwood is a fantastic example of an ancient pollarded tree.

⑨ Brockenhurst

No surrender to modern chain stores here just an old-fashioned high street, Brookley Road, with an independent hardware shop, bookshop, butcher and cafés. It's not uncommon to see cows meandering through

Pollarding in the Forest

Like coppicing, pollarding is a long-established pruning system of forcing a tree to continually produce new growth. In pollarding, cuts are made above the browse line, meaning above where animals can reach, so it was useful in woodlands where animals grazed freely. In ancient times, the new wood would have been used for hedges, fences, houses, firewood and sometimes for animal feed. Branches would be left on the ground for commoners' animals to feed on.

From 1583, attempts were made to stop pollarding as it ruined trees for timber harvesting. The 1698 Inclosure Act prohibited pollarding in oak and beech trees in order to produce tall, straight trees for shipbuilding. That means that any pollarded tree you see today in the Forest is more than 300 years old. Pollarding is still carried out today, but mostly on holly trees to produce feed for ponies.

the centre and for some reasons donkeys love to cluster around cash machines. Glance out a shop window and you might see a pony's face pressed against the glass, peering in.

The North and South Weirs streams converge right in town, often to the inconvenience of motorists unable to cross the **Water Splash**, the ford at the base of the Brookley Road; it's easily bypassed by using The Rise, the parallel street. Open forest lies just beyond the high street at **Beachern Wood**, off Rhinefield Road. The **Rhinefield Ornamental Drive** (see page 58), one of the most popular sites in the Forest, is about three miles away, an easy cycle and obviously short drive.

Church of St Nicholas

Church Lane (away from the main part of the village, on the east side of the A337), SO42 7UB ① 01590 624584 ⓦ www.brockenhurstchurch.com. Volunteers usually sit in the church 14.00–15.00 during summer.

As the oldest church in the New Forest – Brockenhurst is the only New Forest village for which a church is mentioned in the Domesday Book – St Nicholas's Church and its setting boasts a lot of history. Historians believe that the hill on which it stands is partly manmade, suggesting that a pagan temple or Romano–British church once stood here.

If you approach the church on foot (it's a short walk from the station) it's easy to imagine how this church might have appeared to its parishioners hundreds of years ago. Indeed, the words of John Wise, writing in 1862, are apt today:

> For a quiet piece of quiet English scenery nothing can exceed this. A deep lane, its banks a garden of ferns, its hedge malted with honeysuckle and woven together with byrony, runs, winding along a side space of green, to the latch gate.

He would be dismayed to hear the distant road noise but if you can block that out, the lane feels as tranquil as it might have been so many years ago. Wise was less complimentary about the 'wretched brick tower … patched on at the west end' but to the modern eye, it seems fitting. Inside are eight bells.

St Nicholas has an odd shape for a modern congregation; the north aisle, from where it can be a difficult to see proceedings, was built in 1832 to provide seating for the expanding population. The compact building reveals many remnants from its long history. **Roman masonry** is built into the south porch, and just inside the doorway, to the left as you face the door, you can see **Saxon herringbone masonry**. A 12th-century **font** stands in the west end corner of the nave, and nearby behind a curtain a **Tudor arch** spans the entrance to the ground floor of the tower.

The churchyard, which cascades down the hill to the west of the church, is just as atmospheric. The enormous yew tree by the porch, which has a girth of 20 feet, was carbon dated in the mid-1980s and found to be more than 1,000 years old. New Zealanders often come to visit St Nicholas because more than a hundred New Zealand, Indian and other soldiers who died in Brockenhurst field hospitals during World War I are buried here. Brusher Mills, known locally for his snake-catching abilities, also has his final resting place here.

A cycle ride from Brockenhurst

One of my favourite cycle rides in the Forest is to follow the **Rhinefield Ornamental Drive** all the way through until it becomes the **Bolderwood Drive** on the other side of the A35 (four miles) and then all the way to the road's end near **Rockford Common**, a total distance of 13 miles. The short distance boasts almost every terrain the Forest has to offer, from pasture to the dark woods of the ornamental drives with their summertime shocks of magenta foxglove through to the undulating heaths of the west Forest.

Leave Brockenhurst via Brookley Road, then go right on to Burley Road for a short distance until it becomes Rhinefield Road and then leads on to the ornamental drive. After this you simply keep to the same road. You'll need to dismount and cross the busy A35 to continue on to the Bolderwood Ornamental Drive where you cycle through some of the tallest trees anywhere in the Forest. Past Bolderwood, there is a long cruise downhill to the underpass of the busy A31, then it's back up the other side to emerge into open heathland. At the top by **Holly Hatch**, you can see across Fordingbridge all the way to Wiltshire and the hills of Salisbury. If you're feeling peckish, you can cut right across the rough dirt track that leads to the signposted **High Corner Inn** where you can enjoy a drink or basic pub food in the huge garden. The main road then passes through woodland again before emerging into the open, where the **Red Shoot Pub** offers another welcome respite to refresh yourself before retracing your way back to Brockenhurst.

The New Forest Show

New Park, SO42 7QH ℡ 01590 622400 ⓦ www.newforestshow.co.uk.
Held over three days, late July.

I've been to the New Forest Show several times and have yet to leave feeling that I've seen everything. Purchase a programme just inside the entrance and plan the timed events in the rings you most want to see. You can fill in the blanks with the exhibits inside the tents. Programmes vary from year to year but the overall flavour is the same – everyone is here to slow down, have fun and celebrate this region's agriculture and rural pursuits. For three days, the fields behind New Park Manor near Brockenhurst become a mini village which takes several weeks to set up and a full year to plan.

Continuously running since 1921, the show officially incorporates all of Hampshire County but there is a New Forest emphasis, especially if you find your way to the back, away from the commercial bits. The New Forest Corner has everything you need to know, as all the Forest interest groups have stands, including the National Park Authority, the New Forest Commoners Defence Association (whose members churn out wooden signs with your family or house name branded on), the Forestry Commission, the National Trust and the New Forest Breeding and Cattle Society. This is the ideal time to resolve any confusion about who's who in the Forest.

The focus, of course, is the agricultural events which include judging of sheep, horses, and cows in show rings. The animals are housed in huge tents so you can wander in and say hello when they are not showing off in the ring. You can appreciate how many breeds of cows there are generally, let alone in Hampshire and in the Forest. Farmers are happy to chat, especially at the end of the day when things slow down.

Tim Stevenson, of Beechwood Dexters in Bartley, who shows off his cattle explained that exhibiting in the ring can be trying; however, his sense of humour probably makes the experience less stressful. 'You're out there trying to make everything look perfect and of course hoping the judge doesn't look around at that one moment your cow does the wrong thing. You just don't know how she might react when the judge fondles her udder.'

Like other farmers, he clearly enjoys the change of scene and the chance to catch up with fellow Forest workers. 'It's the people you meet; the whole show has such a community feel. You see people that you haven't seen in a long time and everything slows down for a few days.'

One of the best aspects of the show is that it's not assumed that visitors understand everything. Ring events feature running commentary that bridges the gap between ordinary citizens and rural workers. During the very popular 'One Man and his Dog' demonstration, the audience learns traditional sheep dog commands and sees the level of patience required to train a dog to herd sheep. 'We take the dog's natural working ability and extend it,' explained the shepherd. 'In the beginning the dog follows our body language but gradually it learns to obey very particular commands, like "that'll do", when the herding is complete.' She demonstrated with her four-month-old puppy that was already following her body motions and knew instinctively where to move.

Dairy farmers give milking demonstrations throughout the day so that visiting children can understand that the milk they drink doesn't originate in cartons. During 'Horse of the Year' shows, the MC explains what the judges look for and the history of various breeds. Show jumping and other equestrian events take place nearly all day.

An undercurrent of humour runs through the show and the best is found in the Countryside Area where dogs perform impressive and

A wander among the flowers

We stood in an arc, seven of us, hunched over what seemed to me like a giant patch of moss, our backsides protruding in an undignified way. We were inspecting a very tiny plant, so tiny that I would have marched straight over it if Simon, our guide for this Forestry Commission Wildflower Walk, hadn't spotted it.

Simon was so knowledgeable about plants and insects that I asked him what his position was with the Forestry Commission. 'I'm a volunteer,' he explained. 'This isn't how I make my living but I am passionate about the Forest.' Indeed. Who else would give up their Sunday morning to escort a diverse group of plant lovers around a boggy portion of the Forest?

Over the course of the next couple of hours or so, during which time we walked only one mile, Simon's delight with all things Forest was clear. I trotted along at his heels and emerged with a new perspective on the Forest – from the ground up. I had no idea so much was going on beneath my feet. He explained that the teeny, tiny plant in question, a roundleaf sundew, is a carnivore and literally dissolves insects. Moments later he bent down towards another miniscule offering and then continued zig-

sometimes just funny feats. A real crowd pleaser is the terrier race when show attendees are invited to enter their dogs in a race to catch a 'ferret' (all humanely artificial). Getting the dogs to line up is a show in itself.

Even if you are not interested in agriculture, there is something for you here. The shopping is as good as any urban mall with jewellery, handbags, shoes and toys. But of course there is an abundance of farm gear. You'll be convinced you need a handsomely carved walking stick or fur-lined wellies, or perhaps a lawn mower. You can even buy chickens.

A few visitor tips: it can be hot or rainy and either way there are few places to hide. For the remaining 362 days of the year, this is just a giant field with a few isolated trees. So when it rains the mud accumulates, and when it's sunny the heat is merciless. Don't wear open-toed shoes because either the dry dust or the mud will get all over your feet. There is a picnic area if you don't want to be captive audience to the food stalls. Don't get distracted by the rows of shopping that greet you at the main entrance because the heart of the show is in the show rings and the opportunity to chat with participants. Tickets are available online until about two weeks before the show for a 20% reduction.

zagging across the marsh before finally leading us on to a marked trail near Wootton Bridge in the central Forest.

This leisurely contemplation of small wildflowers was completely off my register, but I became enthralled by their identification and learning the origins of their names and the folklore associated with them. During what Simon described as a 'tour of the drugstore of the Middle Ages,' I learned how to use myrica gale as a natural bug repellent; how to identify wild garlic; that sheep sorrel can quench my thirst; and that the root of tormentil might cure colic and cystitis.

When we walked down a path where a gate carelessly had been left open, I saw how much damage the roaming cattle of the Forest can do to flowers and plants. 'This area has been mowed by the cows,' Simon said with a shake of his head. 'There are many flowers we won't see here this year.'

Still, he found plenty for us to examine. We bent down to inspect a cuckoo flower and Simon showed us how the orange tip butterfly lays her eggs on the underside. I left with a sense of awe for the many layers of life that exist in the Forest, each one dependent on the other.

A 25-mile menu

The Pig Beaulieu Rd, SO42 7QL ℗ 01590 622354 ⓦ www.thepighotel.com.

The sign at the entrance to the Pig, a couple of miles east of Brockenhurst, advertises 'kitchen garden food.' That's a tad understated for a restaurant that sometimes has a one-month wait for a table and food that is decidedly gourmet. But the recipe at The Pig works – people come in droves to enjoy the cooking of head chef James Golding and to wander through the gardens of this country house hotel that brands itself a 'restaurant with rooms.'

At first glance The Pig seems like no more than a playground for Londoners who fancy wearing wellies for a weekend but a closer look reveals an underlying Slow philosophy. James is obsessed with growing and raising ingredients in the gardens outside his kitchen and if he can't do that then sourcing them within a 25-mile radius. The buoyant chef grew up in the New Forest and after glamorous stints cooking at The Savoy and other well-known restaurants in London and America, has returned to the Forest to 'give my children the kind of childhood I had.'

As we walked through the immaculate herb, vegetable and fruit gardens of The Pig, James explained his philosophy: 'The gardens are driven by what grows well here and what I like to put on the menu. We grow what's realistic for this climate and I create dishes according to what's ready.'

We stood over rows of blue water mint, lemon verbena and sea kale and then paused at a patch of courgettes with orange flowers draped across the soil. 'Those will be on the menu in the next two weeks,' he said, as he moved on past golden beetroot, pine berries, red celery, borage, sea beet, edible chrysanthemum and broad beans. 'I use every bit of the plant: the beans, the leaf and the stalk.' I didn't know you could eat the leaf of a broad bean until James handed me one and I tentatively popped it in my mouth. We stood there munching in the sunshine as the overwhelmingly fresh flavour burst in my mouth. A few moments later, he passed me a bit of roquette that exploded in a peppery tang.

I began to see why he's so fanatical about using garden ingredients. 'Something grown here that can be picked and prepared in the kitchen in less than an hour will taste infinitely better than something that is picked too early and ripens in transit. It's just the natural breakdown of produce – you lose flavour during transport.'

Much of James's enthusiasm for cooking this way was fostered in early childhood by growing up in a family that celebrated food. 'When I was little my dad used to take us into the Forest to forage for mushrooms. I spent two-thirds of the trip smacking my brother but for the other one-third, I paid attention. When we got home we'd cook what we found and I guess that has just stuck with me. To be able to do that on this level is a dream come true.' He hesitated for a moment before moving on to the next garden. 'Actually much of what I do is an extension of childhood memories.'

His family travelled to Italy when he was a boy, as his maternal grandmother was Italian. He grew up eating smoked meats and the charcuterie that is a mainstay of Italian cuisine. As a chef, he longed to recreate it in the UK. He gets his Saddleback and Tamworth pigs from local pig farmers, Sarah and Roy Hunt of Tatchbury Manor Farm and raises them here until they are ready to eat. 'In the UK we slaughter pigs when they are very lean. I leave them an extra two months in order to be able to make proper Italian-style lardons.'

Even taking pigs to the butcher is an extension of childhood. 'One of my earliest memories is of going to the butcher with sawdust on the floor and meat hanging everywhere – the smell of raw meat was intoxicating. When I came back from New York and settled in the Forest area, I went back to the local butcher, T Bartlett & Son. Of course the sawdust was gone, the meat didn't hang out front anymore and the current Mr Bartlett is the son of the butcher I knew as a boy. We got talking and decided we could work together. Now on a Sunday, my day off, I'm most likely to be found at Mr Bartlett's messing around with charcuterie recipes.'

James also indulges his love of experimentation in his smokehouse, adjacent to where hens cluck around in their pen. His delight was evident as he explained how he bought a garden shed and clad it in New Forest slab wood so it looks like an authentic ancient smoke house. 'The smoker runs on New Forest Oak,' he explained excitedly. 'I arranged a swap in which I give the supplier smoked salmon in exchange for the wood chips.'

As we turned back towards the house, which at one time belonged to the Queen Mother's family, I reflected that it is living closer to its origins than at any time in its recent past. 'This is how people would have eaten in this house at one time,' James remarked. 'The New Forest, despite not being an agricultural area, has offerings from the sea, farms and the Forest. It's exciting to feed people with the riches of this area.'

Food and drink

The Pig Beaulieu Rd (2 miles east of Brockenhurst), SO42 7QL
ⓣ 01590 622354 ⓦ www.thepighotel.com. See page 66 for feature. There
is relaxed sophistication here that's hard to find in the Forest, as well as
really good food prepared from ingredients that mostly come from the
grounds and if not, from within a 25-mile radius. It's not cheap but good
value for the quality and ambience. In summer and into autumn, The Pig
hosts 'Smoked & Uncut', ('uncut' referring to a live performance) Sunday
evening sessions with small bands that play on the lawn while chefs
manning the Mediterranean oven turn out flat bread pocket sandwiches.

Rosie Lea Tea House & Bakery 76 Brookley Rd, SO42 7RA
ⓣ 01590 622797 ⓦ www.rosielea.co.uk. This is where you take your mum
to tea but my 15-year-old son loved it too. The polka-dot tablecloths,
crisps served in tiny matching buckets and flowered porcelain teacups
make this an authentic tea room. The menu has a good sandwich
selection but you really come here for the cakes that are baked in the
kitchen in back. Staff are friendly and eager to please.

The Secret Garden Watersplash Hotel, The Rise, SO42 7ZP
ⓣ 01590 622344 ⓦ www.watersplash.co.uk. This small teagarden tucked
away behind the Watersplash Hotel is a real treat. The marquee, furnished
with armchairs and a fire make it suitable for a coolish day but most of
the seating is on the grass in the garden for a truly authentic summer
afternoon tea. There are tables with fresh flowers and latticed garden
benches. The menu has 'comfort food' of sausage rolls and sandwiches as
well as set afternoon teas featuring homemade baked goods. Open only in
summer, 11.00–17.00 daily. Highly recommended.

Something's Brewing at the Watersplash 61 Brookley Rd, SO42 7RB
ⓣ 01590 624753 ⓦ www.somethings-brewing.co.uk. Not only is this
one of the few places in the Forest that brews really good coffee, but the
atmosphere is relaxed and fresh. Sofas are tucked into corners, armchairs
face the windows and large tables invite conversation with your
neighbour. Local crafts, many of which display the New Forest Marque,
are displayed (and for sale) throughout. There are breakfast specials, a
large menu of sandwiches, soup, salads, and cream teas.

⑩ Roydon Woods

Main entrance at Setley, grid reference SU306004. ⓣ 01590 622708
ⓦ www.hwt.org.uk.

Against the many woodlands of the New Forest, Roydon stands out for the surprisingly diverse landscape of ancient woodland, conifers and streams within its 950 acres. Not too many people come here; I've wandered through countless times and seldom seen another person. You can download self-guided walks from the website and the reserve also runs occasional guided walks with resident rangers. Roydon Woods is also featured in the walk on page 72.

The land, owned and managed by the Hampshire & Isle of Wight Wildlife Trust, has protected status as a Site of Specific Scientific Interest (SSSI). Timber felled during woodland management is used to make fencing, gates and bridges for use in Roydon Woods and other Trust reserves. Oak and softwood products are also sold to the public, as well as venison from deer that are culled. In spring, the dense woods at Roydon burst into colour with some of the best bluebell displays in the area, along with a profusion of other wildflowers and plentiful butterflies. But for me the delight of Roydon is its tranquillity. I live in the heart of the Forest but frequently choose to come here because I always have the sense I am a guest of the deer that remain hidden but watching.

The annual and increasingly popular **Woodfair**, when local woodsmen demonstrate traditional crafts like making besom brooms and walking sticks, is usually held in May and details are posted in advance on the website given above. New Forest Marque members attend and sell their products.

⑪ Setley Ridge Vineyard

A337, 1 mile south of Brockenhurst, SO42 7UF ① 01590 622246
Ⓦ www.setleyridgevineyard.co.uk.

When Paul Girling purchased Setley Ridge Vineyard in 2001, it was in need of tender loving care. When he was laid off from his job as a surveyor in a big London firm, he decided he wanted to return to the area where he'd grown up and make a complete life change. 'Even though I didn't set out to buy a vineyard, I wanted a challenge and I thought the neglected site with its many outbuildings and the beautiful setting presented a lot of opportunities.'

Producing wine in the non-agricultural New Forest is not easy but Paul has taken courses and got help from other English wine producers. Setley Ridge produces five wines: reds, whites and a rosé. The vines are mostly German in origin and therefore suit the cooler climate of the Forest. Weather is obviously one of Paul's greatest challenges but he seems to get enough sun to have become a viable wine producer.

As one of the directors of the New Forest Marque scheme, Paul is dedicated to the concept of supporting local businesses and reducing food miles. 'I don't see myself as unusually environmentally friendly,' he told me as we strolled amongst the tidy rows of early summer grapes. 'It's just common sense. If we destroy our environment we won't have anything left.'

Although Setley wines are not officially organic, he does not use pesticides and only rarely sprays to eradicate mildew, an inevitable side-effect of a soggy English summer. He's even managed to reduce spraying to just one block of grapes. Instead, Paul plants hybrids that are more resistant. 'You can see our environment is healthy because of the varied wildlife we have living here. I regularly see birds of prey, adders, butterflies and a variety of other birds. If we were seriously commercial, we wouldn't have hedgerows but I like them because they attract wildlife and look nice.'

You can't wander by yourself among the vines but if you call ahead, Paul will let you have a look. Free tastings are always available from the farm shop at the front.

There are guided tours for groups of six during which Paul explains the production process from growing grapes to bottling the final product. He includes tastings and if it's a particularly nice day 'we might just settle in under an oak tree and sample the merchandise.' The wine is made on site in the small facility where Paul also produces wines for the Beaulieu Estate.

Food and drink

Setley Ridge wines are sold in the **Setley Ridge Farm Shop** which is located on the A337, in front of the vineyard. Paul's sister, Jane, runs it and she stocks numerous foods from the Forest, many of which hold the New Forest Marque. There are homemade cakes, jams, chutneys, marinades and other sauces. Much of the shop is given over to ready-made meals from Mange-To Go, Jane's company which creates frozen meals with no additives or preservatives. Non-Forest stock is still reasonably local, coming from the Isle of Wight, Hampshire and Dorset.

⑫ Setley Pond and Setley Plain

The very natural-looking **Setley Pond** originated during World War II when gravel was extracted for construction of runways at Stoney Cross,

Sway Tower

From most every angle in the flat heaths surrounding Sway, southwest of Brockenhurst, you can glimpse the 218-foot-tall Sway Tower, also known as Peterson's Folly, a 19th-century structure built by a wealthy judge who had worked in India, retired to the New Forest and fancied a monument to himself using Portland cement. At the time of its construction, it was a record-breaker and it is believed to be the tallest non-reinforced concrete structure in the world. There is no public access; it stands in the garden of a private house in Barrows Lane.

further north near Fritham. I've seen children swimming here, and of course dogs, but mostly this is the local drinking spot for ponies and cows, who often come from quite a distance, nearly always in groups. There is something so fundamentally comforting to see them plodding with purpose across the heath, or along a wooded gravel track.

Setley Pond is also known for the model boats that ply this suitably-sized body of water. The **Solent Radio Controlled Model Boat Club** (*www.srcmbc.org.uk*) has been operating here since 1978 when club members cleared the bottom of the pond to form an island and created a launching area. Sunday mornings, men of a certain age gather to cruise their craft. It's all very sociable – many bring fold-up chairs and set up camp for the day. Because the Club pays a fee to the Forestry Commission to use the pond for sailing boats and because their boats are very expensive, members can seem a bit protective of their turf. But it's fun to watch, especially on a busy day when sailboats vie for space with miniature ferries and noisy power boats. Non-members can sail during Scale Section days on Thursday and Sundays from 10.00 but visitors must consult with club members in order to avoid clash of radio frequencies. There is also the matter of a small insurance fee to pay as stipulated by the Forestry Commission.

On nearby **Setley Plain**, three extremely rare Bronze Age **disc barrows** on the northwest side are the only ones of this type in the New Forest. Mostly found in Wessex, they are distinguished by being round platforms within a circular ditch and bank, and those at Setley Plain include the only pair of overlapping disc barrows in England. They are marked on Ordnance Survey maps as tumuli. The barrows can be hard for the untrained eye to see amid the vegetation, but the

Forestry Commission occasionally organises guided walks to this area in the summer.

Food and drink

Hare and Hounds Durnstown, Sway SO41 6AL ℗ 01590 682404.
A family-orientated pub with decent food and an even better drinking atmosphere. Good selection of ales, including Ringwood and Itchen Valley. Well situated for walks around Sway, Brockenhurst and Setley.

A walk around Brockenhurst, Roydon Woods and Setley Plain

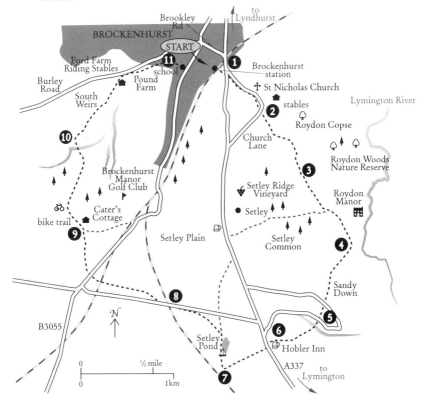

This 6½-mile walk is a splendid mix of deep woods, historic heathland and a New Forest village. If you do it on a Sunday, you might see model sailboats at Setley Pond. You're also likely to encounter deer in Roydon Woods, ponies at Setley Pond and, in summer, cows on the heathland surrounding Brockenhurst. Near the end, you can see one of the pounds used by Agisters to check the health of ponies during regular round-ups. Halfway around, the Hobler Inn, a former pub reincarnated as a modern bistro, has a pleasant garden, although unfortunately it's very close to the busy A337. At the end of the walk, Brockenhurst village has a number of really good tea shops and pubs. A word of caution: at certain times of year the gorse can be high and very prickly. You might not want to wear shorts and proper walking shoes are essential. This walk also can be muddy and wet in places. You can shorten the walk by taking the bus halfway round (see point ❻). The starting point is Brockenhurst station.

❶ From Brockenhurst station, turn right on the A337. Cross the railway and after 30 yards, cross the main road and turn left on to a lane signposted **St Nicholas Parish Church**. Walk up past the church and after it continue on the road half right.

❷ After 200 yards, turn left at the top of the hill across from stables and go through the narrow opening between gates. Walk between fences through **Brockenhurst Park** until the gate marking the entrance to **Roydon Woods Nature Reserve**. The path goes up and down hills, and curves around but is easy to follow.

❸ After a mile, the path intersects a main track. Go left down the hill and pass a red-brick cottage. Continue all the way to the bottom of the slope and then back up another slope for about 200 yards.

❹ At a small clearing on the left, there is a small path opposite, to the right of the main track, signposted Bridleway. Follow this over a small stream and uphill through woods until the ground levels out. Pass through a gate and carry on straight across the turf, with a fence on your left, heading for houses and the road. Pass through a kissing-gate just before the road, then cross the road and go through a second kissing-gate marked 'Hampshire County Council'. Follow the path between hedges until you reach a gate and follow the path down through woods until you reach another gate, just before a small road.

❺ Directly across the road enter woods by a footpath signpost. The entrance is narrow, dark and hard to see. Follow the path a short distance downhill to a footbridge, gate and stile. Continue uphill across the left edge of two fields. At the end of the second field cross a stile into woodland, and follow the narrow path along the left edge of the woods (you will begin to hear the noisy A337) until it emerges on to the right edge of a field.

❻ Reach the A337 and the entrance to the **Hobler Inn** on the left. There is a **bus stop** here if you want to go back to Brockenhurst or reconnect with the green route New Forest Tour bus. Cross the A337 at the Hobler sign and directly across is a narrow entrance to a public footpath, which after crossing a stile, runs to the right of a cottage. After a quarter of a mile, cross another stile to emerge in open heathland.

❼ Head straight on towards a red-brick house with open forest on your right. Pass through a wide gate (usually open) and follow the track around to the right. After 30 yards, cross an intersecting gravel track and follow a wide, open path which gradually narrows and runs to the left of **Setley Pond**. At the end of the pond, continue on the same track until you come to a 'Horseriders' sign facing away from you. You are going to veer left here but before you do, cross the main gravel track and look at the large mound just off the track. This is a circular **Bronze Age barrow**. Go back to the sign and resume the route. Shortly after this, a car track goes out to the main road and a smaller path veers diagonally left. Follow this as it curves gently left down the hill and eventually runs almost parallel with main road.

❽ Cross the road and pass under the railway bridge. At a height-restriction sign (facing away from you) bear half right on a narrow, chalky path that can be hard to see. This path continues uphill at a 'V' angle from the main road. As you climb higher, the path becomes clearer and a quarter of a mile from the original sign, emerges at a railway bridge crossing – you can see the Network Rail signs from a distance. Cross the bridge and walk straight out to the main road. Turn left and walk up to a large road sign with destinations and mileages. Cross the main road (B3055) and pick up a path which bears half right for a quarter of a mile down a slight hill towards a white house in the distance (Cater's Cottage). The path can be hard to see when the gorse is high; you may need to pick your way through, but head toward a gravel track and houses.

❾ Emerge at the gravel track. Turn left towards the houses and walk straight on between Gatehouse Cottage and Cater's Cottage, ignoring a cycle trail which continues to the left. Pass through a barrier on to a track that heads into wooded area. After a quarter of a mile, just before a clump of trees on your left, turn sharp right on to a wide track. This becomes indistinct at times but keep the power lines on your right and after a quarter of a mile the path bends sharply left at which point you will see a bridge (it can be muddy here). Cross the bridge and carry on along the main track as it continues to bend left away from the power lines and into a thicket of trees. After 200 yards, cross another stream by a plank-bridge. Continue straight, up a slight hill.

❿ At a junction of tracks, turn right and walk towards houses. At the barrier, continue on to a gravel track by The Weirs Cottage. Follow this for 300 yards until the main track curves left. Take the smaller track straight ahead, and at the end, by a house, go through the kissing-gate into a field which sometimes has sheep and other times alpaca, to a kissing-gate at other end. (You will now begin to see yellow arrows marking the footpath.) Go through a gate to cut across the corner of another field and then over a stile into a field with a stream on your right. At the other end is another stile. Walk on a narrow path with a fence on your left until another stile then onto a wooded path with a stream on the right. Pass through an iron gate onto the **Ford Farm Stables** road. Turn left to reach the main road and turn right along it, walking on the verge for about 150 yards until you see a dirt track on the right. Peek in here (it can be wet) at one of the **pony pounds**. Go back to the main road, continue in the same direction and walk to the next track where you turn right on the driveway to **Pound Farm**. Cross a bridge at the entrance to the drive and just before the farmhouse, turn left past the hurdle (there is no defined path) and walk along a grassy clearing with a stream on your left. (Note: if this area is waterlogged, go back to the Pound Farm driveway and walk along the main road until taking the first right, opposite Armstrong Lane.)

⓫ After 100 yards, with another footbridge on the left, turn half right on a path that leads toward red-brick buildings and ends at a school. Turn left on to the main road and walk past the school until the junction with Brookley Road. Turn left for Brockenhurst village centre.

Lymington and its coast

As you move towards the Solent, the atmosphere changes distinctly from other parts of the Forest. The major town of this area, **Lymington**, is not part of the New Forest geographically or spiritually, although it is included within the national park. **Yacht enthusiasts** come from all over the world to experience Solent sailing, to which the huge number of moored craft, two sailing clubs and two large marinas attest. You only need to spend an afternoon wandering around the quay or watching seabirds at **Keyhaven** to appreciate the very different essence that ocean air brings. To visit Lymington and say you've been to the New Forest would be inaccurate but to come to the New Forest and not explore the coastal areas around Lymington, especially Keyhaven, would be missing a key element.

⑬ Spinners Garden

School Lane, near Lymington SO41 5QE ① 01590 675488 Ⓦ www. spinnersgarden.co.uk. Garden open Apr–Sep, nursery open Mar–Oct.

Finally, a garden to which an ordinary gardener can relate. Vicky and Andrew Roberts are lovingly restoring this hillside landscape outside Lymington, as well as building up the nursery. It all makes for a pleasant refuge. When you arrive, Vicky is likely to greet you with an information sheet showing seasonal plants. There are only two acres to explore but they will appeal to gardeners because rather than feel intimidated, you can take ideas home and believe that they will actually work. The upper level has pathways that are landscaped to highlight the Forest location – for example, ferns are celebrated. Benches are thoughtfully nestled into pockets of woodland. There are many azaleas, rhododendrons and hydrangeas so the best colour is in late spring and summer.

When Vicky and Andrew bought the overgrown property, they removed an enormous row of Leylandii which has opened up a view across Lymington River valley. Vicky wants to encourage people to stay and enjoy the space so they've put in a small terrace in the middle of the field where you can enjoy a coffee or tea, freshly brewed in the sedum-roofed visitors' cabin. Young children may well home in on the small pond complete with bridge and a bamboo tunnel. The arboretum takes centre stage in the autumn when the Japanese maples offer their yellows and oranges.

Groups are welcome and guided woodland walks take place in spring. The Roberts hope to expand the nursery's tradition of providing rare plants and build a stronger link between the gardens and plants for sale.

⑭ Buckland Rings

Southampton Rd, near Lymington SO41 9HA ① 023 8028 5000. Access is a bit tricky as the entrance is right off the main road; roadside parking is possible in nearby residential streets; the entrance is on the right, by a mileage sign, off the A337 about 150 yards past the Ampress Park roundabout and railway bridge as you head toward Lymington.

Traffic whizzes by this ancient site and it's only when you look closely that you notice the gate leading in to what is one of the best-preserved Iron Age hillforts in this part of Hampshire. Buckland Rings was occupied sometime around 600–100BC, and would have then been treeless. By 100BC, forts in this area had been abandoned.

The ramparts on the eastern side were flattened sometime in the 18th century but on the southern and western side you can clearly see the ditches and banks that once surrounded the six-acre settlement. Just past the entrance off Southampton Road, climb the hillside to see the ditch and corresponding rampart. Although the fort undoubtedly had some military purpose, historians believe that Buckland was an Iron Age community living in roundhouses and using small square buildings elevated on posts to store crops in winter and keep them safe from pests. Locally produced salt also would have been used for food preservation.

What's not immediately clear is that the site is very close to the Lymington River, providing its occupants access to the coast. You can no longer see the river because of the trees planted here during the 18th century when nearby Buckland Manor was landscaped.

⑮ Lymington

Yachting is the flavour of Lymington, not Forest. A bit like Ringwood, it has a split personality of high-end boutiques catering to visitors with boats moored in the harbour mixed with budget-minded retail outlets. The frequency of business closures, particularly in recent years, reflects a reality veiled beneath fancy shops. Like so many towns in southern England, Lymington suffers from chain-store malaise. Independent shops come and go but beneath the surface, the village spirit fights back, especially on Saturday, when market stalls fill the high street (see box, page 79). The **market** is central to Lymington's history, and to a certain degree, its identity. When Lymington was made a town by William de Redvers between 1190 and 1200, he granted the people a charter to hold a market. The wide street was designed to make room for the stalls which ultimately led to the shops that line the street today.

You have to work a bit to find Lymington's character away from the harbour. The best start is at the very fine **St Barbe Museum** (*01590 676969; www.stbarbe-museum.org.uk*). Exhibits on the salt industry, fishing, sailing, smuggling, the rise of tourism, boat building and ancient artefacts found around the Forest give a clear sense of the town's development. Lymington hasn't always been a tranquil sailing port. In addition to salt-making and boat building, one of the town's most flourishing industries was smuggling. Contraband usually consisted of tobacco, alcohol, tea and silk because taxes were particularly high on these items. The illicit trade thrived all along this coast prompting Daniel Defoe to write in 1720 that it was the 'reigning commerce of all this part of the English coast'. Steve Marshall, curator of St Barbe Museum agrees: 'Not only is this area ideal for smuggling in that you have miles of fairly flat, shallow coastland but it was easy to disappear into the Forest with your cargo. Remember that the Forest would have been quite wild and uninhabited then so if you were local, you'd have known where to hide.'

Residents often conjecture about the hidden tunnels that are rumoured to exist beneath the high street around the Angel Inn. Although it's easy to find reports on the internet from people who have seen them, Steve says they are more likely to be drainage tunnels. 'It's a fun local legend, but the facts don't add up. These were drainage tunnels designed to move water down the hill. Of course, it is possible that contraband was moved through them as well; we can't say for sure.'

The one thing that is clear from newspaper reports (on display in the museum) is that smuggling rings could be violent. 'Smugglers had organised and well-armed gangs that wouldn't hesitate to become aggressive towards someone who got in their way.'

The waterfront

At the bottom of the high street, a cobbled pedestrian way curves down to **Lymington Quay**. Although lined mostly with souvenir and ice cream shops, this is the most appealing part of town. Children might enjoy swinging nets off the main pier in hopes of catching crabs and it's a pleasure just to sit on the wall and watch boats come and go. A small fleet of fishing boats is still based at the quay, mostly catching oysters and shellfish from the Solent. Oysters have long been a mainstay of Lymington fishermen; shells periodically found during excavations in the high street show that they were a staple from medieval times until the 19th century. Today, they serve as winter income for fishermen when other fish are scarce.

A short walk away from the port towards Keyhaven along **Bath Road**

If it's Saturday, it must be Lymington

Lymington market Every Sat 08.00–17.00; some traders begin to pack up at 16.00.

Steve, a trader at Lymington market has been manning a stall for 47 years. 'I started here when I was nine years old, helping my dad. He first started in the days before cattle grids and the day began with clearing up after horses. Now the worst days are the windy ones because you can't keep anything down. Wind is much worse than rain.'

Every Saturday, Steve stands behind his stall surrounded by tidy stacks of brightly-coloured jigsaws. He has one of the prime pitches in the middle of town, a reflection of his longevity here. Together with his two brothers, their merchandise covers a healthy stretch of Lymington High Street. 'We're like a department store,' laughed Steve. 'Over the years we've sold bedspreads, toiletries, hardware, gifts – whatever the market demands at any given time.'

There has been a market in Lymington since 1250. Today Lymington is one of the few markets in southern England that hasn't been privatised but is still run by the local council. That means pitch rental is cheaper and the market has retained an old-time flavour.

More than 90 stalls run the length of nearly all of Lymington High Street, from the top of the hill that comes up from the harbour, to the church. In the early days, the market was much smaller and focused on food, but has now expanded to include jewellery and other items.

According to traders, the high street has changed as much as the market. 'Most of the family businesses have gone,' said Steve. 'And as for the early cafés, they're gone too. The tourist information centre was a school – it has all changed.' He points to a high street clothing retailer. 'That was an agricultural merchant.' But there is no regret in his tone, just practicality. 'You have to change with the times.' Steve's good nature obviously keeps him going even when he must get fed up packing and unpacking the van every Saturday. 'I like coming to Lymington. I still get people asking after my father and regular customers who come looking for a special product. Another good thing is that the shops realise we bring customers in whereas they used to think we took business away. Now shopkeepers even come out with a cup of tea occasionally. We're all working together in tough times.'

(which is all land reclaimed from the river in the early 19th century) reveals a cross-section of Lymington history. Just past the town quay, the **Berthon Boat Company** employs about 200 people and produces pilot boats, used to guide large ships in and out of ports – as well as lifeboats and yachts. The company continues a long-established Lymington tradition that began with Thomas Inman, a yacht builder who came to the town in 1819 and introduced the idea of pleasure boating on the Lymington River. After about half a mile you arrive at **Bath Road Recreation Ground**, a wide-open grassy park that borders the Lymington River. The benches that line the waterway are a fine place for a picnic as you overlook the dense array of masts that stand as thick as a Forest woodland, while passing Isle of Wight ferries give the eerie impression of gliding on air. Further across the car park, just outside the **Royal Lymington Yacht Club**, stands one of the original gas lamps

Coastal birding

Two Owls Birding Regular courses and bespoke trips and walks for beginners and more advanced observers with Nick and Jackie Hull ① 01202 620049 ⑩ www.twoowlsbirding.co.uk.

The joy of the Solent Way between Keyhaven and Lymington is that it's a perfect cycle trail without cars and a view of the Isle of Wight. Or so I thought until I visited it slowly with Nick and Jackie Hull, two intrepid birders who know so much about winged creatures that my head was whirring when I left them after three hours.

Although the human population here swells in summer, feathered creatures prefer winter so this area is jammed with waders in December, January and February. In autumn I walked with this couple, and they found plenty. 'You can come two days in a row at any time of year and see different species,' explained Jackie. 'There are many which just stop in for a rest if there is a storm brewing and then move on to Europe or Africa in their migration.' The Solent is on the migration path of millions of birds and ducks.

I expressed surprise at how far some creatures fly to and from here. Nick smiled. 'Swifts will go to Germany for the day if they sense a storm,' he explained. 'They're smart enough to fly through the rain to get the back end for good feeding conditions.'

installed in the town in 1832. Not long after, Lymington was one of the first towns in the south to convert to electric street lamps, but oddly in 1933, the town switched back to gas. Reportedly this was because of the high cost of electricity but might it have been because several town leaders held shares in the Lymington Gas and Coke Company?

A bit further west is one of Lymington's most special features, the **Sea Water Baths** (*01590 678882; www.lymingtonseawaterbaths.org.uk*), a huge outdoor saltwater swimming pool beside the Lymington Town Sailing Club. The town briefly flirted with the hope of becoming a spa under the auspices of the Lymington Bath and Improvement Company in the 1830s. The pool and bath house (now the Lymington Town Sailing Club) were built at a time when ocean bathing was believed to be unusually restorative. People did come for a while but Lymington's spa dream was not to be realised, as saltwater bathing went out of fashion.

It was fun sighting different species but the highlight of the day was realising the ecological significance of this relatively small stretch of coast. As we walked along the elevated path, wind whipping around our ears, Nick described the migratory habits of many birds. 'We're starting to see species settle here, like the little egret that used to live only in the Mediterranean or north Africa. It might be due to global warming or it might be a natural cycle, we don't know.'

We stopped to watch a black-tailed godwit. 'They come from Iceland,' Nick explained as he lined up a perfect view for me in his telescope. 'They start moulting there, fly here for the winter, and then finish changing here to their drab winter colours so that they look quite different than when they left. Long ago, this confused naturalists who thought they were different species.'

'As technology becomes more sophisticated, we are learning more and more but we're only at the tip of the iceberg in terms of what we can know. In the old days they shot birds to learn, now we put trackers on. So, for example, now we know that our cuckoos spend the winter in Chad.'

Nick's broad historical perspective made me think not only about the importance of Keyhaven in the broader ecological sphere but also about how these remarkable migrations take place right in front of us while we rush past. Next time I come out here, I'll replace the bicycle with a pair of binoculars.

The huge, unheated pool is usually open from May to September but it closes on occasion so phone ahead. It's wise to wear plastic shoes as the bottom can have sharp shells or even nibbly crabs.

Lymington-Keyhaven Nature Reserve

① 01590 674656. Parking is easy at public car parks in Keyhaven or Lymington and there is also very limited parking at the end of Lower Pennington Lane and in Lower Woodside, at the bottom of Ridgeway Lane.

If you continue out to the sea wall, you can walk the five miles to Keyhaven and even further on to Milford as part of the Solent Way (see page 88). Maps are available from the tourist information centre in New Street. The route passes through the Lymington-Keyhaven Nature Reserve, which begins just past the marina in King's Saltern Road. The marshes here were the heart of Lymington's salt-making industry in the 18th century and the reserve contains the best-preserved examples of medieval and later salt workings in southern England (see box, page 83). An audio tour, *Seabirds and Saltpans,* talks about both the salt industry and wildlife living on the reserve and can be downloaded from www.newforestnpa.gov.uk. It is narrated by Pete Durnell, manager of the site for Hampshire County Council.

The path passes alongside Normandy Marsh and Maiden Dock before coming to **Moses Dock** where stand the only two remaining sea-salt works in the entire country. Just after this point, it's possible to exit the reserve at Ridgeway Lane from where a path leads to the Chequers pub, or you can continue to **Keyhaven**.

Birdwatchers come from all over the UK and even further afield to enjoy the abundant flocks that reside in the 500-acre reserve during winter. 'From December through February there are about 10,000 birds living here,' said Pete Durnell. 'One of the things that makes the reserve special is that we are still very much part of the New Forest. In summer, commoners graze ponies and cattle here which enables us to maintain the shore grasses at an optimum level for birds that return home each winter.' These include brent geese, kingfishers, black-tailed godwits and the largest settlement of pintail ducks in Hampshire.

Diversity of habitat is another key feature of the reserve. 'Lagoons, reeds beds, saltmarshes and mudflats make an unusual combination that provides rich feeding ground for so many species.' Year-round residents include curlews, little egrets, redshanks and ringed plovers. This area, along with Hurst Spit, is continually changing. In the 19th century, grasses began colonising the mudflats here, reaching their peak in the 1920s. Now as they begin to die back, marshes are returning to mudflats.

Birds aside, this is a memorable spot for a coastal walk. 'This is one of the few places along this coast that's accessible to the public – most of it is privately owned,' said Pete. The stretch to Keyhaven is along a gravel track that is wheelchair- and pushchair-accessible. In contrast to a bracing walk along the coast, the paths at Keyhaven reveal the intricacies of mudflats and grasses as well as providing a clear view of the Isle of Wight.

Salt-making at Lymington

It's hard to believe as you walk in this tranquil setting that 200 years ago this area was a busy industrial centre as sluice gates opened and closed, wind pumps whirred and boiling houses steamed. Salt-making was Lymington's most important industry for hundreds of years and there is evidence that salt may have been manufactured here in the Iron Age. The first record of it is in the Domesday Book of 1086, which lists six salterns at nearby Hordle. The industry peaked around 1760 when there were 149 pans working. In 1800, 4,000 tons of salt were produced and exported to the Channel Islands, Newfoundland and Scandinavia. Wealth from the industry is reflected in the Georgian mansions around Lymington High Street.

By today's standards it seems like an extraordinarily laborious process but ingenious in its method of harnessing nature. At high tide, seawater filled feeding ponds. Sluice gates drained water into evaporation pans where it stayed until wind and sun evaporated most of it. Wind pumps then pushed the remaining brine into holding tanks from where it was fed into boiling houses, where fires under metal pans boiled away the last bit of water. The remaining salt crystals were then transferred to buckets and carried away.

The obvious question is, especially if you visit on a characteristically soggy English day, how could that method be practical in this climate? And the answer is that it wasn't. Lymington ultimately lost out to the more efficient production methods and the cheaper rock salt being produced in Cheshire, as well as extremely high taxes on salt. By 1850, production had ceased.

Food and drink

Chequers Inn Ridgeway Lane, SO41 8AH ① 01590 673415 ⓦ www.
chequersinnlymington.com. This 16th-century pub was around in the
days when the Salt Exchequer Offices were nearby. It's a friendly pub
where dogs wander in and out and sailors share tales at the bar. Standard
pub fare, but the atmosphere's jolly, especially in summer when barbecues
are held in the courtyard.

Goodall's Strawberry Farm South Baddesley Rd, SO41 5SH ① 01590
679 418 ⓦ www.goodallsstrawberries.co.uk. Strawberries have been
grown on Goodall land in Lymington for a century. From 1 May to mid-
July you can pick your own strawberries in open fields and polytunnels.
They grow eight varieties to extend the season. As the season progresses,
broad beans, raspberries, cherries, blueberries and sometimes potatoes are
added to the pickings. A lot of fun, and lovely views of the harbour.

Fine Food 4 Sail Bath Rd, SO41 3YL ① 01590 677705 ⓦ www.
finefood4sail.co.uk. Some local landlubbers don't even know this café
is here because of its location just outside of downtown at Berthon
Marina. Sailors arrive by boat so it has a yachting flavour appropriate for
Lymington. Oddly there is no water view but the blond wood tables and
banquette seating compensate. Closed Mondays.

S & J Shellfish Snooks Lane, SO41 5SF ① 01590 688 501 ⓦ www.
sandjshellfish.co.uk. Shellfish supplier somewhat bizarrely situated in a
barn in the middle of a field. But they are known locally for supplying
super-fresh crab and lobster, caught in Lymington waters. They supply
many local restaurants and will provide shellfish to campers and others
staying nearby. New Forest Marque members. Phone ahead with your
order.

The Ship The Quay, SO41 3AY ① 01590 676903 ⓦ www.theship
lymington.co.uk. Location, location, location right on the water. If you're
lucky enough to snag a waterside table in summer, you'll have a view of
yachts and children catching crabs at the wharf. Food is decent and the
atmosphere is lively.

Stanwell Hotel Bistro High St, SO41 9AA ① 01590 677123
ⓦ www.stanwellhousehotel.co.uk. One of the few restaurants that has
withstood the test of time. A more cosmopolitan atmosphere than those
nearby but unlikely to have many locals.

Willow 60 High St, SO41 9AH ① 01590 670000. The cupcakes in the
window should be tempting enough but this café that's part of an interiors
shop is stylish and somehow soothing. Best for just coffee and cake.

⑯ Milford on Sea

Somewhat appropriately for this old-fashioned seaside village, the post office in Milford shuts for lunch. Local jokes focus on the average age of residents as north of 70 and indeed, there is a preponderance of OAPs. But it might just be that they have the last laugh.

For when the summer glare fades and the ice cream crowd returns home, Milford dons a charm of a bygone age. In the late 19th century, Colonel Cornwallis-West of Newlands Manor, a grand estate, had ambitious plans to make Milford a fashionable seaside resort akin to Eastbourne. He added the 'on sea' to Milford's name and began to develop the Hordle Cliff area, between Milford and Barton-on-Sea. Unfortunately due to a typhoid outbreak and lack of funds, his dream never came true. The village has a feeling of having been passed by, but that rather adds to its appeal.

Recently Milford has been attempting to launch itself as a foodie destination. The restaurant **Verveine**, connected to the fishmonger of the same name, draws people in, as do the cookery days offered by its head chef, David Wykes. Instruction is also available at **The Granary Kitchen Cooking School** (*www.thegranarykitchen.com*) run by Christian Rivron. The annual **Milford on Sea Food Week** is in its infancy but shows promise with lots of food-related activities for one week around Easter, including cooking demonstrations, various opportunities to meet with local producers and a large food fair with stalls on the village green and the high street.

David Rogers and his wife Lucy of Vinegar Hill Pottery, both of whom grew up in nearby Lymington, say that the reputation that Milford has as a retirement community is only partly accurate. 'It is true that there are a fair number of older people here,' said Lucy. 'But there is a whole other side that most people don't see. The school is blossoming and there are lots of young families who have figured out what a fantastic lifestyle Milford offers.'

In another nod to a bygone age, Milford has **Pleasure Grounds**, 14 acres of ancient woodland with trails that run along the Dane Stream, parallel to the coast. They are located at the western end of the village, conveniently next to the car park. You can walk through the pleasure grounds (enter from Park Lane) to New Valley Road and on into **Studland Common Nature Reserve** to follow further footpaths along the river. It's not as remote as the Forest by any stretch but if you're here and you're looking for a woodsy experience, this is a good place to have it. It's also a good combination with the cliff-top walks of the area.

Vinegar Hill Pottery

Milford on Sea SO41 0RZ ① 01590 642979 ⑩ www.vinegarhillpottery.co.uk.

David Rogers's hands smooth the spinning clay into a perfect round shape as his pottery wheel rumbles and whirs. 'Our set-up just kind of evolved because all aspects work so well together,' he said, referring to the multi-faceted business of pottery studio, classroom and B&B that he and his wife, Lucy, run in Milford. Dave, an accomplished artist in his own right, decided to start teaching his craft to people who came to stay at their B&B. Or was it people who came to stay at the house became interested in taking pottery classes? Either way, it's a splendid mix and Dave still finds time to create his signature brilliant blue tableware and earthy casserole pots which are on display in the upstairs gallery.

One- and three-day courses limited to six people take place throughout the year and Dave will arrange special group events. The small studio stretches to accommodate six wheels so that each student has their own station. 'Many people tend to do evening courses when they study pottery but it's just not long enough,' said Dave, as we climbed the steps to his gallery showroom. 'But we add in the fun of some really good food. We break for coffee and cake in the morning and then after guests have had a good turn at the wheel, we head in for a relaxing lunch.' Potters are fortified with a feast prepared by a family friend.

∽∞∾

Food and drink

Beach House Park Lane, SO41 0PT ① 01590 643044 ⑩ www.beachhouse milfordonsea.co.uk. A good place to come after walking the coast between Lymington and Barton-on-Sea or as a destination in summer for the terrace overlooking Christchurch Bay and the Isle of Wight. The two small dining rooms have a bland, hotel ambience but the views are worth it.

Braxton Gardens Lymore Lane, SO41 0TX ① 01590 675 488 ⑩ www.atbraxtongardens.com. This plant nursery tucked away off the A337 is a quirky place for a light lunch or afternoon tea. In summer, tables are set up in the small manicured gardens and if it's cold, the conservatory has a wood-burning stove. Closed Mondays.

Mr Pink's Church Hill, SO41 0QH ① 01590 642930. How could you visit the seaside and not have fish and chips? Mr Pink's, something of an institution in Milford, is the place to do it. Sit on a bench on the village green to enjoy your meal or walk down to the beach.

Pebble Beach Marine Drive, Barton-on-Sea BH25 7DZ ℗ 01425 627777 Ⓦ www.pebblebeach-uk.com. A few miles past Milford in Barton-on-Sea, Pebble Beach has the ultimate seaside terrace on a summer day with views of the Isle of Wight and yachts in the Solent. It's an expensive treat but worth it for the view and the fish menu perfectly prepared by Pierre Chevillard. The only questionable aspect is the not-so-background music.

Verveine High St, SO41 0QE ℗ 01590 642176 Ⓦ www.verveine.co.uk. Many restaurants tout use of local ingredients but it is the mantra at Verveine. Virtually every ingredient on the menu is sourced from within the New Forest. The menu is a simple blackboard of today's catch (usually plentiful) with a choice of four sauces and accompaniments that brilliantly play with your expectations. The small kitchen is just a few steps from the dining area and it's an informal, friendly experience. Good-value set lunches. Highly recommended.

⑰ Hurst Castle

℗ 01590 642344 Ⓦ www.hurstcastle.co.uk. Open daily Apr–Sep, weekends only Nov–Mar; English Heritage.

Getting to Henry VIII's fortress is as much fun as the castle itself. You can walk the mile-long stretch of Hurst Spit from Hurst Pond or take a ferry from Keyhaven; the most satisfying option is to walk out and get the ferry back, or vice versa. If you walk one way and ride the other, park in Keyhaven car park. The ferry landing is a short walk away and Hurst Spit is about a quarter of a mile further along Keyhaven Road. For a longer walk, park at the seafront in Milford to walk the full length of the Spit.

Walking towards Hurst Castle provides such a close view of the Needles and the Isle of Wight (it is only three-quarters of a mile away from the castle) that it seems as if you will walk straight on to the island. The stones on the sandbar produce a satisfying crunch with each step, although it can get tiring, so wear solid shoes. Waves either pound or lap the pebble beach, depending on the wind.

Henry VIII knew that he had angered Catholics in Europe when he divorced his first wife, Catherine of Aragon, and dissolved the monasteries, so he set about building a string of coastal defences at each end of the Solent. Calshot was the first, and construction began in 1539 and Hurst was the last to be completed in 1544.

Walks along the coast

Technically, it's possible to walk west from Milford all the way to Bournemouth. The website www.visitmilfordonsea.co.uk lists walking options. Closer to home, the three-mile walk from Milford to Barton-on-Sea on a combination of hard path, grass and earth, can be an invigorating seaside experience, especially off-season when colder winds blow. The area by **Hordle Cliff Beach** is ideal for pushchairs and wheelchairs and you are treated to unfettered views of the Isle of Wight and on a clear day, on to the Purbeck Hills, Hengistbury Head and Christchurch Harbour. Summer has its own charms, even if predictable ones. Children race in and out of the waves and couples stroll hand-in-hand across the bumpy shingle.

I heartily recommend walking the length of **Hurst Spit** even if you don't plan to visit the castle. Just before the spit, a bird hide is tucked away between the Marine Café and black council sheds. Children might like to fish for crabs off the wooden bridge by **Sturt Pond**. (Crabbing equipment is available in Milford at Milford Models or the newsagent.) The **Solent Way** (*www.solentway.co.uk*) a 60-mile footpath linking Milford with Emsworth Harbour, just beyond Portsmouth, begins here. It's nine miles to walk to Lymington via Keyhaven. In the shelter of the Isle of Wight, you won't experience the onslaught of ocean winds but instead this journey offers quiet contemplation of marshes and abundant birdlife. If you don't want to walk back to Milford, you can take a bus from Lymington (*www.wdbus.co.uk*). You can use the public car park at Sturt Pond; parking is free along Saltgrass Lane, but watch the tide, as this road is known to flood.

This is the best castle in the area for young imaginations, and bodies, to run free. There are many large, vacant rooms, narrow staircases and dark, dank cellars to explore. The flip side of that freedom is that there is little explanation of rooms so you might want to spring for the audio guide or purchase the small handbook. Children won't necessarily mind the absence of historical explanations; the two huge Victorian guns and many passageways to explore are diversion enough.

When you enter, turn left to see Henry VIII's portion of the circular castle, designed to defend against land or sea attack. The drab wings that extend from the original Tudor circular castle were added in the 1860s, when the only perceived threat was from the sea. Only the west wing is open to visitors. Several defence updates took place over the years: during the Napoleonic Wars in 1794 and again in the 1850s and 1860s. During both world wars, the castle was garrisoned. An interesting remnant of life for the more recent troops is the recently restored **Garrison Theatre** in the West Wing, possibly the only surviving garrison theatre from World War II. Shows are still held here during the summer. English Heritage does a good job maintaining the military flavour; even the lavatories are modelled on the Garrison latrines of 1870.

When you climb to the top, and see the views of Hurst Spit and the Isle of Wight, it becomes clear how difficult this land would have been to protect but what an ideal vantage point the fortress had. Both rooftops display interesting plaques describing what the scene would have been like in different periods of history. In the West Gunner's office is an excellent exhibit on the conservation issues facing Hurst Spit.

Inside the grounds of the West Wing, the café has outdoor tables sheltered from the wind. If you plan ahead, I'd recommend bringing a picnic and sitting outside the castle walls to enjoy the view of the Solent or marshes of Keyhaven.

When longshore doesn't drift

For a lesson in how protection of one stretch of land can negatively affect other areas, head to Hurst Spit. Sea walls and groynes installed in recent years at Milford to prevent cliff erosion have prevented by-products of erosion from travelling to the spit.

The mile-and-a-half-long spit, formed some 7,000 years ago when the Isle of Wight separated from the mainland, was getting pushed further landward by wave and tide action and was gradually disappearing. In 1989, a major storm shortened the spit by nine feet in one night; this prompted ecologists to campaign for rebuilding the spit. A model was built in a wave tank to test the effects of wave action, tides and currents in order to determine the best preservation method. Rocks were brought in to build up the spit and to preserve this guardian of the western Solent.

Annual maintenance should preserve the spit but it will continue to move. Without it, the saltmarsh nature reserves would be devastated, the castle would become an island, Keyhaven and Lymington would be vulnerable to flooding (as witnessed in 1989), and the northwest part of the Isle of Wight would suffer severe erosion.

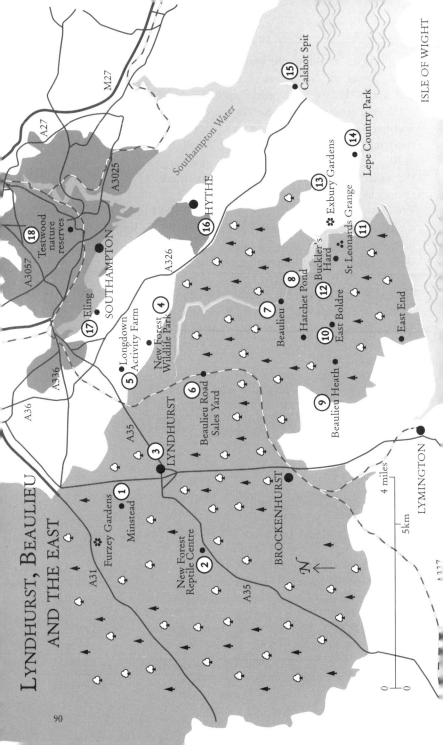

LYNDHURST, BEAULIEU AND THE EAST

ISLE OF WIGHT

M27

A27

A3025

Testwood nature reserves (18)

A3057

A3336

A36

Eling (17)

SOUTHAMPTON

Southampton Water

HYTHE

(16)

(15) Calshot Spit

Exbury Gardens (14)

(13)

Lepe Country Park

Longdown Activity Farm (5)

New Forest Wildlife Park (4)

A326

St Leonards Grange (11)

Buckler's Hard (12)

Beaulieu (7)

Harchet Pond (8)

East Boldre (10)

East End

Beaulieu Heath (9)

A35

LYNDHURST (3)

Beaulieu Road Sales Yard (6)

Furzey Gardens (1)

Minstead

A31

New Forest Reptile Centre (2)

A35

BROCKENHURST

N

LYMINGTON

A337

0 ____ 4 miles

0 ____ 5km

3

LYNDHURST, BEAULIEU AND THE EAST

From 'capital' to coast, the eastern part of the New Forest National Park is wonderfully diverse in landscape and aura. You have to work a little harder here to escape the tourist crush but when you do, you are richly rewarded with distinctive communities, wildlife experiences and landscape within a relatively small area.

Lyndhurst, the Forest's unofficial capital and tourist mecca, can be hard to love but it's saved by the presence of the New Forest Centre and library and proximity to open Forest. If you don't have much time, or are unfamiliar with the Forest, Lyndhurst is an ideal starting point, especially if you want town facilities (think how often it rains) as well as nature walks. Very nearby are some of the Forest's most beguiling places, such as **Swan Green**, **Bank**, **Emery Down** and **Minstead** with its enchanting **Furzey Gardens**. Apart from Setley Pond near Brockenhurst, the only other place where **model boats** are allowed is at Fox Hill Pond, a smaller manmade pond north of Minstead and Emery Down; access is from Andrew's Mare car park, the last left before the A31 on the road from Emery Down. **Cycling** on the quiet lanes around here is perfectly feasible although there is some traffic. The Forest cycle network has trails from Lyndhurst to Brockenhurst.

Much of this area is comprised of the **Beaulieu Estate**, a 7,000-acre estate privately owned by the Montagu family and its ancestors since 1538 when land belonging to **Beaulieu Abbey** passed into secular ownership. Wherever you are in Beaulieu, you're probably on land belonging to Lord Montagu. You're also walking on the very ground where the monks of Beaulieu Abbey once prospered.

While the dominance of the Estate might not be apparent to the casual visitor, local business owners tell tales of strict regulations imposed by Lord Montagu, right down to the size of signs and their lettering. Aside from the hassles for locals, the restrictions help the area maintain its pristine looks. The clock really does seem to have stopped here, especially on lazy days when cows lounge on the grass by the mill pool and donkeys nuzzle tourists at the edge of the Beaulieu Estuary.

Further east are some odd juxtapositions. Rugged beaches at **Lepe** and **Calshot** challenge the bland suburbs of Southampton up the road, while the bucolic village of Exbury is just moments away from unphotogenic sprawl. In the shadow of Fawley oil refinery, rare birds preen and parade and seem all the more thrilling because of their backdrop.

The rocky coastline of Calshot and Lepe gradually gives way to the tamed walkways of **Exbury Gardens**, which in turn differ dramatically from the open forest of East Boldre and Beaulieu Heath. East End has its own distinct landscape of sleepy country lanes bordered by distant ocean and fields. If you are caught between a love for Forest landscape and the sea, East End offers a balance.

World War II left its mark on Beaulieu and its coast. Remnants of the three runways built at Beaulieu Heath in 1942 are used today as bike trails and for launching model aircraft. Streets and bridges were widened to accommodate tanks (especially evident in the village of Pilley); private homes along the Beaulieu River and coast were requisitioned to serve as headquarters and training camps for members of the Special Operations Executive, a secret spy-training unit; and the Beaulieu River became crowded with landing craft and barges in preparation for D-day. Troops that trained at Exbury left there for Normandy; for many, Beaulieu River was their last view of England. Exhibits at Beaulieu Palace, Buckler's Hard, Lepe and Calshot provide excellent background and remind us that not all that long ago the Forest coast was overshadowed by war, a far cry from the blissfully peaceful atmosphere that pervades today.

Accommodation

Acres Down Farm Minstead SO43 7GE ℡ 023 8081 3693
Ⓦ www.acresdownfarm.co.uk Ⓔ enquiries@acresdownfarm.co.uk. The very basic camping facilities here offer a chance to stay on a working commoners' farm with cows, sheep, pigs and chickens. Payment is according to the size of your tent so can be excellent value. There is a small farm shop and cream teas in summer. Simple toilet block and showers for small extra fee. Open all year but no reservations.

Dale Farm House Dibden SO45 5TJ ℡ 023 8084 9632
Ⓦ www.dalefarmhouse.co.uk. Well-situated for Southampton Water and the Exbury/Lepe coastal area, this superior farmhouse B&B has direct access to the Forest. The immaculate garden has a terraced seating area with barbecue overlooking an adjacent field (which unfortunately has a massive electricity pylon but you get that anywhere hereabouts). It is well offset by the charming hosts and their professional standards which include well-presented rooms and a hotel-style breakfast room. Five average-priced en-suite doubles, two of which can be enclosed to make a family suite and one double with private bath. The whole house can be rented for family parties.

East End Arms Main Rd, East End SO41 5SY ℡ 01590 626223
Ⓦ www.eastendarms.co.uk. The five small rooms above the pub in this sleepy corner of East End are stylish and welcoming. The two superior rooms differ from the three standards only in size – for those who want a bit of extra space, they are essential. Numbers 2 (superior) and 3 (standard) have the best views over a long expanse of field leading to the Forest. Breakfast is served in the pub dining room or outside on the terrace where donkeys frequently peer in. Good value if you want low-key hotel style; only a bit more expensive than a standard B&B.

Fleetwater Farm Bed & Breakfast Newtown SO43 7GD ℡ 023 8081 2273 Ⓦ www.fleetwater-farm.co.uk Ⓔ heather@fleetwater-farm.fsnet. co.uk. It feels like coming home when you step into the Aga-warmed kitchen of the old farmhouse at Fleetwood Farm, where B&B is offered. Before long the resident cocker spaniels will smell you out and befriend you for the rest of your stay, so this is not a place for non-dog lovers. Breakfast is served in the flagstone dining room. The two average-priced large doubles are well-presented; one has a prettier view over the garden, the other has an enormous bathroom. Also a small double with a private but not en-suite bath. Across the way, another bedroom is available in a separate cottage that used to be the study of the writer and TV presenter Jack Hargreaves when he owned the house. The bathroom for this room is in the main house. Well-behaved dogs (that get along with the owner's dogs) are welcome but children are not. The Trusty Servant pub in Minstead and Furzey Gardens are within walking distance.

Luttrell's Tower Eaglehurst, Southampton Ⓦ www.landmarktrust.org. uk. Here's a chance to relive smugglers' history in this Georgian folly overlooking the Solent towards the Isle of Wight, now an upmarket self-catering let sleeping four and owned by the Landmark Trust. The basement tunnel leads directly to the beach, possibly a remnant of its original owner, Temple Luttrell, an MP who reputedly was also a smuggler in the late 18th century. Upstairs virtually every inch of living space has a view of ships entering and leaving Southampton. All rooms have restored chimney pieces and there is elegant plaster and shellwork in the top room.

Master Builder's Hotel Buckler's Hard, Beaulieu SO42 7XB Ⓣ 01590 616253 Ⓦ www.themasterbuilders.co.uk Ⓔ enquiries@themasterbuilders. co.uk. This was the home of the master shipbuilder, Henry Adams, between 1749 and 1805. The hotel, which describes itself as providing 'quirky luxury', comes into its own when the museum closes and the guests have the hamlet of Buckler's Hard virtually to themselves. Eight rooms in the main house; number 20 has a corner view over the river and a four-poster bed. The 18 rooms in the Henry Adams Wing are separate from the hotel and cost less than the expensive luxury of the house. A self-catering cottage in the centre of the hamlet sleeps four. Both half-board and B&B are available, as well as lots of package offers which can be quite cost-effective. Dogs are allowed in some rooms.

Mill House B&B Palace Lane, Beaulieu SO42 7YG Ⓣ 01590 612347 Ⓦ www.beaulieubandb.com Ⓔ info@beaulieubandb.com. A privileged chance to get an inside look at living on the Beaulieu Estate. The front of this 16th-century house opens directly on to busy Palace Road but at the back, the small garden and breakfast patio overlook Beaulieu River. The old-fashioned furnishings of the one double and two twin-bedded en-suite rooms might not appeal to everyone but the house is filled with character and the hosts are delightful. Average prices.

Minstead Village Shop Minstead SO43 7FY Ⓣ 023 8081 3134 Ⓦ www.minsteadshop.co.uk. If you want to feel a part of village life, you'll appreciate this tiny cottage for two located behind the village shop on the village green and managed by the very friendly shop owners. The basic bedroom and small kitchen are slightly dark but you have your own barbecue area, bike storage and continental breakfast in the village shop. It's available as B&B or self-catering; prices slightly more than local B&Bs.

Roundhill Caravan & Camping Site Beaulieu Rd, Brockenhurst SO42 7QL ① 01590 624344 Ⓦ www.campingintheforest.co.uk. The open, grassy spaces amid the 500 pitches of this Forestry Commission campsite make this child-friendly. Set in a particularly appealing part of the Forest surrounded by woodland and heath with plenty of ponies wandering through. No electricity, but good toilet and shower blocks. Close to Hatchet's Pond for fishing and access to bike trails. Local cycle companies will deliver cycles upon your arrival. Booking essential in peak season; well-priced for area. Open April–September.

Whitemoor House Southampton Rd, Lyndhurst SO43 7BU ① 023 8028 3043 Ⓦ www.whitemoorhouse.co.uk Ⓔ whitemoorhouse@tiscali.co.uk. From the stuffed toys on beds to the jolly welcome of owners John and Stephanie Drewe, it's the personal touches that make Whitemoor an enjoyable place to stay. A highly professional B&B that feels like a small hotel, the house is on the very busy route between Ashurst and Lyndhurst but that's the price for being within walking distance of Lyndhurst's facilities as well as the Forest; there are six average-priced en-suite doubles. The Drewes are dedicated to conservation; discounts are given to guests who arrive on bicycles. They will collect guests (or send a taxi) from Brockenhurst or Ashurst train station. No credit cards, no children under 12. Open mid-February to October.

Lyndhurst and surrounding areas

Lyndhurst is on the doorstep of the wilder north Forest, not too far from the coast and handily placed for pottering around and sightseeing generally. Several animal-centred activities are nearby and the three highlighted in this section are informative and fun, especially the **New Forest Wildlife Park**, which is beautifully landscaped. The town itself is something of a mixed bag. At peak times, the pavements and shops overflow with people, and traffic gridlock is notorious; most locals avoid the major roads into town during the summer. But Lyndhurst does have redeeming features. Its connection with royalty is evident at **Queen's House** and the view of **St Michael's and All Angels Church** from Bolton's Bench is quite special, while exhibits at the **New Forest**

Minstead as inspiration

The path which the young clerk had now to follow lay through a magnificent forest of the very heaviest timber, where the giant bowls of oak and of beech formed long aisles in every direction, shooting up their huge branches to build the majestic arches of Nature's own cathedral.

Sir Arthur Conan Doyle *The White Company* 1891

Probably Minstead's best-known resident was Sir Arthur Conan Doyle, who bought his second wife, Jean, a cottage here for her birthday. The house, Bignell Wood, now has been enlarged and modernised and is not visible from the road. The author's affection for the area is evident from the words above describing Minstead wood.

Conan Doyle was heavily involved in spiritualism, and Bignell Wood is reputed to have hosted spiritualists' retreats but his daughter, Jane, denied this in an interview before her death, saying that it was purely a place of relaxation. She reported that he was friendly towards the gypsies that lived in the woods around the house and recalled him going off to visit them.

The success of Sherlock Holmes convinced Conan Doyle that he could

Centre open an excellent window on the Forest for newcomers and old-timers.

This area certainly has money; if the Maserati dealership in the high street isn't clue enough, Lyndhurst frequently pops up in 'most expensive town' surveys. Lime Wood, one of the priciest hotels in southern England, is just beyond the town centre. You could argue that these extravagances diminish the New Forest flavour of this area.

But town pavements change abruptly to woodlands and heath around Lyndhurst. The ancient parish of **Denny Lodge**, just to the east is mostly comprised of heathland with some 90 Bronze Age barrows. Lyndhurst Old Park, the large deer park created by Norman kings, was supplanted by 'New Park' up the road at Brockenhurst in 1484. You can still walk where bygone horsemen rode, across Park Pale, an earthen bank and internal ditch that enclosed the medieval deer park, and along the time-worn track of Beechen Lane, once a regular route for travellers between Denny Lodge and Lyndhurst.

quit practising medicine and be a full-time writer. But he preferred many of his other writings, according to Dr Roger Straughan, author of *An Elementary Connection*. Conan Doyle's many published works included historical fiction, verse, plays, short stories and books on spiritualism. The first section of the 1891 novel, *The White Company*, takes place in the 14th-century New Forest. 'Well, I'll never beat that!' he is reported to have said when he completed it. He also penned a short story, *Spedegue's Dropper*, about a cricketer who practised bowling special high-pitched lobs in the New Forest by slinging a cord between two trees.

The spot under the tree in Minstead Churchyard was not the author's first resting place. At his death in 1930, he was buried (allegedly vertically) in the garden of his Sussex home in Crowborough but when Jean died, he was exhumed and moved to Minstead where she had always wanted to be buried.

'He was the archetypal Englishman,' said Dr Straughan, during a speech at the New Forest Centre. 'It's appropriate that his final resting place is under an oak tree at Minstead in the New Forest that he loved so well.' But Straughan pointed out that it's just as well that the writer lies 'a discreet distance from the church,' as he was at odds with the Church of England for most of his life.

① Minstead

On the surface, it is little more than a sleepy place with a green and containing a shop, post office and pub, but for such a small village, a surprising amount is going on in Minstead. Its thatched houses and local walks make this somewhere well-worth making a point of wandering out to if you're in or around Lyndhurst, not least for its links with Sir Arthur Conan Doyle.

At the **Minstead Study Centre** (*023 8081 3437; www.minstead. hampshire.org.uk*) tucked away in the woods just outside Furzey Gardens, Jane Pownall and Chris Townsend host groups of schoolchildren aged roughly eight to 11, for a week of immersion in rural life and a lesson in how to 'live lightly on earth.' Programmes for the wider community are limited at the moment but it's worth checking the website for periodic 'early years' courses and open days, as well as unusual workshops hosted by outside instructors. The site, including the impressive sustainable dormitory, is sometimes available for group rentals.

All Saints Church

Just up the hill behind the village green stands All Saints Church, where fans of Sherlock Holmes make pilgrimages to see the final resting place of **Sir Arthur Conan Doyle**. He has a plum position beneath a giant limb of an oak tree at the far edge of the burial yard. Someone has thoughtfully placed a pipe on the tombstone. A bench is waiting for you to have a quiet read of one of Conan Doyle's stories of the master sleuth.

Coppicing: reviving an ancient tradition

'My earliest memory is of my grandfather bringing me out to the Forest where he worked as a woodsman,' said Dave Dibden, 57, a modern-day coppicer. 'I was very small and he would place me on the back of his Irish wolfhound from where I'd watch him work.'

Coppicing is cutting a tree at its base to promote growth of several different shoots rather than one stem. Almost immediately after making the cuts, new green shoots emerge which, after many years, will become trees. By continuing to make cuts in the stool (the base from which new growth occurs) a coppice generates a continuous supply of new wood. This ancient form of forest management provides both fuel and raw materials, as well as encouraging diverse habitats.

I was privileged to walk with Dave where he has cleared and coppiced Pondhead Inclosure, a previously neglected woodland near Bolton's Bench in Lyndhurst. (The entrance is off Beechen Lane, south of Lyndhurst.) By hand, he and Forestry Commission volunteers have carved out generous trails through dense overgrowth of brambles and trees. Using old maps, Dave is working to restore this inclosure to how it would have been in the 18th century. The Commission let the land go wild until 2004 when Dave was asked to manage it through coppicing. 'When I started here, the old trails from the 1970s were completely overgrown – they were like dark tunnels.'

Dave begins by clearing and coppicing a small area and fencing it off temporarily to prevent animals from grazing and to allow new growth to develop, which in turn provides habitats for important insects and butterflies. He continues to nurture new patches while the old ones mature and begin to host still more varied species. 'I do the coppicing here in a seven-to-ten year rotation. In this way you always have different levels of habitats.' Dave uses all the wood that is cut away to

The church itself is a pleasing mishmash of different time periods. The oldest relic is the **Saxon font** which was lost during the Reformation, perhaps buried for safekeeping, and then dug up in the Old Rectory garden and placed back in the church in 1893. The Norman doorway dates from 1200, while the 16th century saw the arrival of the oak pews and three-tiered pulpit – with the top level preaching, the middle for Bible readings and the bottom level where the clerk stood to say the

make crafts in the style of ancient woodsmen. He sells his hand-carved walking sticks, bird feeders and gardening materials at local fairs and to private clients, as well as practising the ancient craft of charcoal burning.

Coppicing has been used since Neolithic times (about 4000BC) and was the most common form of woodland maintenance in Britain until the 1800s, and at one time was considered the only way. But in today's world of pesticides and quick fixes, this ancient art is taking on a new significance – a viable system that honours a rural tradition.

'Because coppicing is an ancient system, butterflies and birds have become reliant on us to sustain their environment in this way,' explained Dave. 'If the forest becomes overgrown and dark, species that require open light will die out and cause others further up the food chain to die.'

We stopped to examine an old bit of honeysuckle hanging from a tree branch. 'We can encourage the white admiral butterfly by leaving these old bits of honeysuckle. The caterpillar lays its eggs on the old bits because there are no berries and birds won't be attracted and therefore won't eat the caterpillar.' Suddenly Dave pointed ahead on the path. A small butterfly, a pearl border fritillary, zig-zagged above the tiny flowers that line the path. Dave was visibly pleased. 'They haven't been in this area since the 1960s. Because butterflies don't travel far, once you lose them, you really lose them. But they're coming back now that the magic light is allowed in.'

As we neared the end of our walk, Dave hoisted himself on to a gate and perched there, looking as natural as any of the creatures that live in his woodland. 'Today we live life trying not to be part of the natural world but we all are. You learn so much from nature and one of the most important lessons is to go at its speed. You can't force it.'

Dave can arrange tours for groups (*023 8087 2679; www.coppice-products.co.uk*).

'Amens' after prayers. The timbered upper gallery dates from 1700 and the bell tower is Georgian. Off the sanctuary is a private pew which was built for the residents of nearby Malwood Castle who enjoyed all the comforts of home including a fireplace and a private door through which their dinner could be delivered.

Furzey Gardens

☎ 023 8081 2464 ⓦ www.furzey-gardens.org.

The playful and fanciful layout of Furzey will stay with you long after you have left. What distinguishes these enchanting gardens is that they are tended by the learning-disabled students of Minstead Training Project who work here as part of their training to develop confidence, independence, and social and work skills. The Project is a nearby residential and day programme to help young learning-disabled people reach their full potential.

'Working here gives people with learning disabilities a place where they fit in and can contribute which is especially important because they often feel excluded from other walks of life,' said Pete White, head gardener and horticultural instructor. 'The students like that they make a difference to the landscape and to visitors' experiences here. That then translates to greater confidence and independence in daily life.'

Pete, who has directed the work in the gardens for 12 of the 23 years for which he has worked for the charity, believes that the community spirit and joy of empowering the disenfranchised is conveyed to visitors. 'The underlying ethos of the entire project enables visitors to enjoy a spiritual sense when they are here,' Pete told me as we strolled along the narrow pathways that necklace across the sloping land. 'It's broad strokes here, not the fine details you might see in a more formal layout. We don't want to bludgeon nature into submission but gently draw it out.'

In the children's area, African-style round houses are linked by tunnels and walkways. The **Typhoon Tower**, a viewing platform with a thatched tower, has beautiful views over the Forest towards the Isle of Wight. Best of all, Simon Sinkinson, the thatcher responsible for the enchanting structures, has carved some 30 fairy doors, hidden among flowers and trees.

The gardens originally were planted in 1922 by Bertram Dalrymple, a native Scot who built Furzey House, now a Christian retreat next door. He brought in topsoil to replace the native gorse and clay substructure and then proceeded to plant exotic rhododendrons and azaleas that plant hunters of the day were bringing home from the Himalayas and Australasia. After Dalrymple's death, the land and buildings began to decline. In 1972, the property came on the market with approval granted to demolish the 16th-century thatched **Cobb Cottage** at the entrance. Fortunately, a trustee of the Furzey Gardens Charitable Trust, which now runs the site, swooped up the land with the idea of restoring the cottage and the 1920s flower-beds. The cottage, built from boat timbers from nearby Lymington boatyards, has now been restored to provide an authentic vision of how people would have lived.

Furzey has been encouraging more children to visit and as Pete and I sat on one of the many benches, we watched youngsters running on the wide lawn near the entrance. 'We also are hoping to make everything more accessible to disabled people, which is a challenge on this hilly and often damp site.' Admission is free to the disabled and their carers.

As much as Pete values caring for people and flora, he also enjoys nurturing a landscape that contains so much history. 'We've dug up bits of Roman pottery that could be from the Roman site that was near here. We're also working on an extensive replanting scheme based on original records. We know when everything first went in and as original growth begins to fade we can regenerate by taking seeds and cuttings.'

Next door is a café with outdoor tables and an area where plants grown by students are for sale. Not surprisingly, Furzey also encourages bee populations and an interactive display teaches visitors how beehives work.

As I left Pete, he was off to work with his second session of students for the day. The afternoon's work included clearing undergrowth and laying wood chips, a job that requires tractors. 'That's always a popular one,' Pete said with a smile and a cheerful wave.

A short walk around Minstead and Furzey Gardens

This circular stroll of just over a mile around Minstead takes you to all the key sites. Begin at the Trusty Servant pub by the village green; roadside parking as well as a village car park.

❶ With the Trusty Servant behind you, take the road along the right side of the village green, passing the war memorial at the end of it. Soon take the path to the right of the churchyard and go through the gate to the path with a hedge on your right and wire fence on your left. Go

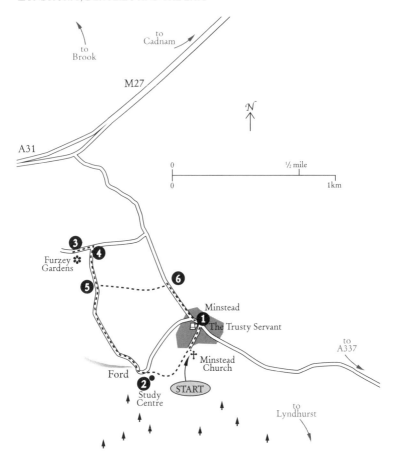

through a second gate and down the hill through woodland (the area to the left has been coppiced).

2 Leave the wood through a kissing-gate and turn right towards the main road. Across the road and a bit to the left you'll see a sign towards Furzey Gardens. Cross the main road and turn right into this lane. Walk up the hill past Minstead Study Centre on the right.

3 Continue on past the first lane on the left and walk all the way to the second lane on the left, signposted **Furzey Gardens**.

4 After about 100 yards you reach the entrance to the gardens. After visiting the gardens, retrace your steps, turning right when you leave the gardens until you reach the grassy triangle where you bear right. Continue on to the right on to the main road.

❺ After 100 yards, you'll see a small opening in the hedge on the left, with a stile and footpath signpost. Cross the stile and walk downhill through a field with a hedge on your left. Cross a wooden bridge over a small stream and climb over a wooden fence with a Hampshire County Council yellow arrow footpath symbol. Continue uphill through the next field with a hedge on your left.

❻ Cross the final stile and turn right on the main road, which you follow to the Trusty Servant pub on your right.

Food and drink

Minstead Village Shop & Tea room ☎ 023 8081 3134
🖳 www.minsteadshop.co.uk. Armchairs in the window overlooking the village green and tables outside in summer. Simple offerings but a pleasant stop in the centre of the village.

The Trusty Servant ☎ 023 8081 2137 🖳 www.thetrustyservant.co.uk. Classic pub food in an historic setting. Just on the edge of the village green, the pub building has been here since the 1800s and the pub itself since 1903. Notice the sign which depicts a man with donkey's ears, a pig's snout and stag's feet. The snout has padlocked lips to indicate discretion. A similar painting of this odd creature hangs at Winchester College and it is believed that the College once owned the land on which the pub now stands. In summer, the large garden and terrace tables are almost always full and the small but cosy interior is a pleasant Sunday lunch spot.

② New Forest Reptile Centre

Holidays Hill, off A35, 2 miles southwest of Lyndhurst 🖳 www.new-forest-national-park.com/new-forest-reptile-centre.html. Open Easter–end Sep; free (modest parking charge). Grid reference SU269072.

Visit this small but worthwhile reptile centre on a sunny day, partly because the snakes and lizards hide when it rains and partly because the walks in the surrounding woods are particularly lovely. This is an ideal place to compare the ancient and conifer woodlands that make up the New Forest. A marked one-mile **Reptile Trail** passes through a conifer woodland with very tall Douglas Firs, glades and a pond. On the other side of the centre, towards the A35 a stream meanders through an area of ancient woodland, comprising oaks and beeches.

Reptiles particular to the New Forest, including toads, frogs and various types of snakes are housed in a series of outdoor enclosures. Adders are common in the Forest, but tend to slither away when they sense humans approaching, so this gives a much better opportunity to see them. The Reptile Centre has successfully bred and reintroduced sand lizards, which were extinct in the New Forest by 1970.

One of the best features here has nothing to do with reptiles. Webcams, or rather **nestcams**, operated by the Royal Society for the Protection of Birds, are trained on nests of birds of prey from April to September. If you come in the spring, you might get to see chicks being fed or just squawking about. In the hut where the videos are displayed, there is information about birds of prey and ground-nesting birds. The staff of volunteer rangers is knowledgeable and friendly.

③ Lyndhurst

The people of Lyndhurst ought, I always think, to be the happiest and most contented in England, for they possess a wider park and nobler trees than even Royalty. You cannot leave the place without going through the Forest.
John R Wise *The New Forest: Its History and Its Scenery*

Lyndhurst has been considered the capital of the Forest since William I designated it as such in 1079. In subsequent years, when kings and queens visited William's hunting ground, they stayed at the royal manor, now known as the Queen's House (which changes its name depending on the gender of the monarch). Although royalty has long departed, it still feels like the capital as the Forestry Commission is now headquartered in **Queen's House** and the **Court of Verderers**, which oversees commoning practices, is right next door. You can't just wander in but the New Forest Centre often leads tours as part of their excellent series of walks (see page 106). The Court's monthly sessions are open to the public ten times per year.

The town's central **location** at the junction of two major thoroughfares, which have evolved from medieval tracks, also plays a role in its capital distinction. Southampton Road (A35) which runs between Southampton and Bournemouth, and the Lyndhurst Road (A337) which goes from the M27 and Cadnam on to Lymington in the south (changing its name along the way) converge here. The long traffic queues that build up in the one-way system are a testament to the power of the Verderers who have vetoed any efforts to install a bypass.

Guardians of an ancient way of life

The walls of the ancient Court of Verderers in Lyndhurst are adorned with deer heads, including two skulls with interlocking antlers facing the same way – a remnant of two rutting bucks which became entangled and ultimately lay down to die. They serve as reminders of the New Forest's founding as William's royal hunting ground and the Verderers' original role to uphold Forest Law on behalf of the Crown.

Nowadays, this venerable panel safeguards commoners' rights rather than those of the Crown. No prosecutions take place in this chamber, although in past days those who broke Forest law were spared no mercy. Present-day sessions are really more like open forums with contentious issues left to private consultation among members.

Anything that will affect commoners' work, including a major event in the Forest, has to get past these ten overseers. They consider proposals for development or any action that will influence the Forest, ranging from the installation of power lines to the designation of cycle trails. Sessions are held on the third Wednesday of each month during which time anyone can present a proposal.

Positions are unpaid, and presumably undertaken from sheer love of the Forest and the opportunity to influence its management. Five are elected by commoners and five are appointed by government organisations that are responsible for Forest management. Verderers often visit the Forest to investigate land under question but day-to-day field work is conducted by Agisters who look after commoners' stock (see page xi).

If you manage to visit on one of the guided tours run by the New Forest Centre and step back from the awe of this historical setting, you'll notice that it's all a bit shabby. There is frequently talk of a spruce-up but perhaps Forest business is deemed more important. On one wall hangs a small stirrup which also dates from the harsh days of Forest law. Dogs too small to fit through the 'Rufus stirrup' were nevertheless deemed large enough to be a threat to the King's deer and had their paws maimed so they couldn't chase them. Dogs small enough to pass through the stirrup were spared.

The term 'Verderer' derives from the French word, 'vert', for green, meaning that these agents were official keepers of the green. It's still an apt name as they have huge influence on retaining the character and borders of the Forest.

Congestion is particularly bad in summer when it can take more than 30 minutes to pass through town on the A337.

'A tourist honeypot' is how Forest management views Lyndhurst and it's easy to see why. The town has an impressive array of restaurants, cafés and gift shops. Within minutes you can be deep in the Forest, as John Wise so eloquently pointed out. Just a few steps from the high street, **Bolton's Bench** is a distinctive hill capped with a yew tree, leading out to the heathlands of White Moor.

Along with the official buildings at the top of Lyndhurst High Street, the 19th-century **church of St Michael and All Angels** presides from its lofty position atop a prehistoric manmade mound. This is the third church to stand here, the present one succeeding Saxon and Georgian versions. The structure, designed by William White, was financed by subscriptions from local people who felt the existing Georgian house of worship was too small. But when it was constructed between 1860 and 1870, some locals decried the many-coloured bricks as too garish – especially on such a visible point in town. By the altar is a fresco of wise and foolish virgins in which local people were depicted as biblical figures. It was painted by Lord Frederick Leighton who was excited to try out his new acrylic paints; its gold lettering sparkles when the sun shines on it. Alice Liddell, the inspiration for the Alice in *Alice in Wonderland*, lived nearby and is buried in the churchyard. Her grave displays red and white roses in a tribute to the royal gardeners in the book who painted white roses red. The church bell ringers practise on Thursday nights, as do those of nearby Minstead.

Lyndhurst comes in to its own at Christmas. Bolton's Bench is often frosty white and I can't think of too many places that wear sparkly lights so well. That endless traffic queue seems to die down a bit and even if you do get stuck in it, it's worth it when you see the high street all dressed up for St Nicholas. Lyndhurst becomes a small town with a heightened feeling of anticipation and a rich sense of the past.

New Forest Centre

It would be easy to mistake the New Forest Centre for a simple tourist information office but it is so much more. Housed in the same building as the main tourist information centre in the Forest, the New Forest Centre is run by an independent charity started by a group that believed people should be educated about the Forest.

'William the Conqueror was in effect the Forest's first tourist – he designed it as his personal playground,' Suzie Moore, Education Development Officer told me. 'Tourists are an important source of income in the area but they can also cause problems such as feeding and petting commoners' livestock, trampling vegetation, disturbing ground-nesting birds and of course increasing traffic congestion. The potential conflict between tourism and preservation can be balanced by fostering visitors' understanding of how the Forest works.'

To that end, much of the building is dedicated to a **museum** with exhibits about the flora and fauna in the Forest; New Forest ponies and how they maintain the landscape; a model of Beaulieu Road Sales Yard; the history of the Forest; and ongoing conservation efforts. In addition to the permanent displays, changing exhibitions explore topical themes. During school holidays, the Centre holds drop-in activity days for families at which children make crafts and examine elements of the Forest; these are a lot of fun. Even people who have been visiting the Forest for years will gain a deeper understanding of the Forest's intricate workings.

One unusual exhibit is the **New Forest Embroidery**, a 25-foot-long tapestry designed by Belinda, Lady Montagu of Beaulieu in 1979 to commemorate the 900th anniversary of the creation of the New Forest. The colourful work depicts the most important historical events in the Forest set against a backdrop of Forest flora and fauna.

An excellent introduction to the Forest is to go on one of the **Open Forest Walks**, easy two-hour explorations taking place near Lyndhurst with a National Park ranger who discusses all aspects of Forest management; they run periodically on Thursdays throughout the year. The Centre also arranges bespoke walks for groups for a minimum charge. **Wednesday night talks** with guest speakers on various themes are ideal for those who want to delve into a particular aspect of the Forest. These often have a link to current exhibitions at the centre.

The **Christopher Tower Reference Library** is included in the price of a ticket to the museum. Its extensive collection includes classical works published from the 18th to the 20th centuries, as well as natural history books, travel guides, maps, art, postcards, photos and information on individual Forest towns, including a lot of material on the New Forest's military history. To appreciate how the Forest looked in the 19th century, view the Burrard Albums (available on disc): Charles Burrard lived at Holmfield House, a large house off Lyndhurst High Street, and apparently gave each of his six daughters an album made up of paintings of the Lyndhurst area including Emery Down, Stoney Cross, Minstead and Southampton. The librarian, Richard Reeves, will assist with historical queries but you need to phone ahead to arrange an appointment. Membership of the New Forest Centre entitles visitors to free unlimited entry to the museum for one year and discounted admission to special events.

The **Gift Shop** by the entrance is quite entertaining with a diverse selection of Forest books, crafts and toys.

Food and drink

Greenwood Tree 65 High St, SO43 7BE ℡ 023 8028 2463 ⓦ www.the-greenwoodtree.co.uk. The enormous menu should be enough to satisfy every palate. The specialty is sweet and savoury waffles which means there are odd but fun presentations of full English breakfast or meatballs with tomato sauce on top of a waffle. There are also regular meals and takeaways.

Herb Pot Bistro Lyndhurst Rd, SO40 7AR ℡ 023 8029 3996 ⓦ www.theherbpot.com. It feels as if Alan Rogers and Shelley Richards invited you to their home when you dine here. Shelley, who once worked as a chef at Windsor Castle, toils away in the kitchen while Alan warmly welcomes guests. It's a slow leisurely meal well worth the wait because food is stand-out for the area. Good for vegetarians and open for breakfast. Closed Sunday and Monday.

Imperial China 18 High St, SO43 7BD ℡ 023 8028 3398 ⓦ www.imperialchinalyndhurst.co.uk. The atmosphere is a bit dated but service is efficient and it's above-average Chinese food. One of the high street's better choices.

Lyndhurst Tea House 26 High St, SO43 7NH ℡ 023 8028 2656 ⓦ www.lyndhurstteahouse.co.uk. The large open room is an uninspiring space but you can enjoy scones and generous slices of cake for an afternoon respite. The enormous choice of meals and all-day breakfast is ideal if some people in your group want lunch but others want afternoon tea.

Oak Inn Bank SO43 7FE ℡ 023 8028 2350 ⓦ www.oakinnlyndhurst.co.uk. Just outside of Lyndhurst, the Oak is one of the great New Forest pubs: although many come here to dine, it has managed to retain its old-fashioned pub feel. On a sunny day, the garden is an idyllic spot for lunch and the inside is cosy with a lively atmosphere on winter evenings. Booking advised.

Waterloo Arms Pikes Hill SO43 7AS ℡ 023 8028 2113 ⓦ www.waterloo armsnewforest.co.uk. One of the better pubs in the area located in the tiny hamlet of Pikes Hill, just outside Lyndhurst. Nice layout with a comfy bar area and plenty of tables to choose from. The garden is spacious.

④ New Forest Wildlife Park

Deerleap Lane, Ashurst SO41 4UH ℡ 023 8029 2408 ⓦ www.
newforestwildlifepark.co.uk.

The collection of mammals and birds at this wildlife park is eclectic in the extreme. But it all makes sense when you consider that most of the animals here, like the deer, owls and foxes, live in the open forest and others like the lynx, wild boar and wolves did so many, many years ago. As for the wallabies, they are a playful extra, though there are some living wild in the UK according to owner, Carol Heap. Carol and her husband Roger are dedicated to otter preservation so there are a lot of otters playing around. They are the only people to successfully breed the giant otter in this country, and there is a growing family here. If you have never seen a giant otter before, you're in for a surprise: they are big.

The Heaps also are committed to wildlife rescue and educational programmes. The park is one of the few centres in the country with a licence to look after rescued wild otters; each year Carol and Roger take in some 15 to 20 orphaned Eurasian otter cubs, which are kept separate from the public and then carefully released into the wild. Injured or abandoned deer, hedgehogs, foxes, owls and badgers are also looked after here.

Even if you're not a fan of wildlife parks, you may well enjoy this because its setting celebrates the Forest. Trails snake through woodland past enclosures, some of which are nestled deep in the trees. If you visit during term-time at a quiet time of day, you're likely to be completely alone for some soul-enriching viewing.

Deer and wallabies roam freely (not in the same section) so it's not unusual to find certain beasts on the same walkways as people. The deer are extremely tame – so much so that during my visit one snatched my map and consumed half of it before I had the wherewithal to snatch it back. Other creatures like the lynx and wolves can be harder to see. 'British wildlife is secretive and elusive, so it's difficult to enable visitors to see all the animals without stressing them out,' Jason Palmer, Animal Manager told me. 'That's why we have frequent feedings and interactions throughout the day.'

Just before the deer and owl section, a large play area offers outdoor fun in a wooded setting. Climbing frames and basket swings are spread out in a large open space padded with woodchips for safe landings. There are picnic tables and a view of the deer which live nearby. It's all done in a tasteful, understated way, better than many child-oriented attractions.

⑤ Longdown Activity Farm

Deerleap Lane, Ashurst SO40 7EH ☏ 023 8029 2837 ⓦ www.longdownfarm. co.uk.

It's hard to tell who is more important at Longdown Activity Farm: animals or children. The experience is all about introducing youngsters to farm life and they love it. Interaction sessions, including bottle-feeding goat kids and calves or just holding baby rabbits and ducks, are held throughout the day. Even the most cynical will be charmed by the sight of children cradling guinea pigs and chickens or better yet seeing the joy on adults' faces when they do the same. Wet-weather attractions slightly detract from the emphasis on farm life but if you're travelling with little ones and it's rainy, the large soft-play area, a barn filled with hay bales and roofed trampolines are welcome entertainment. In better weather, outdoor table-tennis and go-karts are a fun way to let off steam, and tractor and pony rides run all day during summer weekends. One of the most distinctive activities is the opportunity to look for freshly laid eggs and then carry them to the farm shop, located at the entrance.

⑥ Beaulieu Road Sales Yard

3 miles south of Lyndhurst, by Beaulieu Road railway station on the B3056 ⓦ www.nfls.org.uk/saleyard.htm.

Most of the year, the holding pens and auction ring at Beaulieu Road Sales Yard stand empty next to the Beaulieu Road railway station. But roughly five times each year the yard springs to life with sales of New Forest ponies and sometimes donkeys. All sold at auction are registered either with New Forest Pony Breeding and Cattle Society or New Forest Commoners Defence Association so buyers know they are getting the real thing. Some 90% of the ponies sold at auction come directly from the Forest but others come from members in other parts of the country. Sale prices have been declining in recent years but efforts are underway through controlled breeding to improve value.

Even if you have no interest in purchasing anything, if you're in the area on the day of a sale, it is definitely worth a visit. You can wander about freely and look at the animals (sometimes donkeys included) as they await their turn in the ring. At the pre-show, sellers can show their best ponies to serious buyers. 'The breed is good for riding because of their gentle nature and exposure to a variety of situations,' said David Readhead, chair of the New Forest Livestock Society.

Criteria to be an authentic New Forest pony are strict. Only those whose parents are both registered as purebred in the stud book can be considered purebred. There is no minimum height requirement but animals must be no taller than 58.25 inches. Official New Forest ponies can be any colour but piebald, skewbald or blue-eyed cream.

The auction is a lively, sociable atmosphere as groups of commoners gather to talk about problems with their animals' health, Forest issues, or just the weather. Grab a perch in the spectators' seats around the auction area and watch the action. It's fun to hear the auctioneer conduct the sales in guineas (price is converted to pounds upon purchase and the difference offsets the levy instilled by the auctioneer). It's also entertaining to try to guess what the prancing ponies will fetch on the open market – it's not always the show winners that achieve the best price.

Beaulieu Estate, Buckler's Hard and East End

The village of Beaulieu and much of the surrounding area is virtually synonymous with the **Beaulieu Estate**, the largest private estate in the Forest.

The land has been owned by the Montagu family since 1538, when Thomas Wriothsely, an ancestor of the current Lord Montagu, purchased 'the whole close of Beaulieu' from Henry VIII after the Dissolution. The boundaries of the Estate originally mirrored the 10,000 acres of the Great Close of Beaulieu Abbey until the 1950s and 1960s when the southwestern portion around Sowley was sold.

I have a fondness for Beaulieu, although there's no getting away from the fact that it's a huge family attraction which gets big crowds in high season. Beneath the frenzy, the essence of the village shines through: on an early morning when mist rises above the mill pond with Palace House in the background and you'd swear a medieval monk will appear on the lawn; on a busy Saturday afternoon when cows, oblivious (or not) to the long string of cars held hostage, insist on standing on the road markings leading to town; or during a quiet walk in the woods between Buckler's Hard and Beaulieu village when you hear only birds singing and see glimpses of the river through the trees.

For a bit of drama, windswept **Beaulieu Heath** is both historic and peaceful. It's a popular place to walk but even so, you can easily find yourself alone with the many ponies that tuck themselves into clumps of gorse. To the south, the Isle of Wight makes a pleasing backdrop but further east, the towers of the Fawley oil refinery are a reminder that the Forest borders serious industry. It's hard to walk or cycle along the remnants of the airfield here and not wonder what World War II pilots must have thought as they manoeuvred their planes on to the runways built during the war.

The peaceful country lanes around the **Beaulieu coast** offer superb **cycling**. My favourite routes are along the quiet roads of **East End**, from where you view the sea and expanses of fields. The public is granted rare access to the coast down Tanner's Lane which is off of Lymington Road, but it's a small stretch. The loop from Beaulieu through **Buckler's Hard** and on past the ancient site of St Leonard's is an excellent ride thanks to the relative lack of traffic. The B3054 is a lovely flat stretch through Beaulieu Heath but this also is a main route through the Forest, so is probably unsuitable for children. The cracked and sometimes bumpy tarmac cycling trails at Beaulieu Heath are reclaimed from a World War II airfield.

⑦ Beaulieu

Abbey, Palace House and Motor Museum ① 01590 612345 Ⓦ www. beaulieu.co.uk.

Beaulieu's history begins with the abbey. After Henry VIII's dissolution of the monasteries, the village population grew from the settlement of workers who had provided services to the abbey and people who had sought sanctuary within its walls. Modern roads leading from Beaulieu grew up from the ancient paths that monks used to stay in touch with their local and more distant landholdings. Nothing seems to have changed in hundreds of years although shop occupants come and go with the times. Today, estate-owned cottages, which are identifiable by their dark red doors and diamond logos, are rented to local people and former employees of the Estate.

Beaulieu's permanent population is about 840, but in summer the village swells with thousands of tourists who mostly come to visit the Motor Museum, Abbey and Palace House; indeed, Beaulieu's Motor Museum attracts more than 300,000 visitors each year. Lord Montagu's detractors cynically comment that the village of Beaulieu is nothing more than a money-making enterprise and according to one local resident 'unless you bring income to the Estate, you can't live here'. Lord Montagu admits it is a 'corporate enterprise' in his book *Gilt and the Gingerbread,* but one that looks after its employees and grew from his deep love of the Estate and sense of obligation to his title. Whatever the inner workings, Beaulieu is a memorable place to visit and crammed with intriguing history that is kept alive by the throngs of tourists.

One way to enjoy the largely private land of Beaulieu Estate is by joining one of the activities run by **New Forest Activities** (*01590 612377; www.newforestactivities.co.uk*), located in the old Forge midway along Beaulieu High Street. The outdoor activity company runs activities including archery, treasure trails, combat games, canoeing and kayaking (see box on page 114).

Beaulieu Abbey

Beaulieu Abbey is the foundation of this entire area. Legend proclaims that King John founded the Abbey after dreaming that the monks attacked him in retaliation for taxing them heavily. He began to fear the wrath of the religious community and in 1204 gave the Cistercians New Forest land to establish an abbey. John's pious son, Henry III and then later Edward I granted more land and by the end of the century there were some 200 men living and working within the abbey walls.

The location was perfect. Its proximity to the river meant that heavy stone from the Isle of Wight and Normandy, as well as marble from Purbeck, only had to be carried about 300 yards to reach the construction site. Some 30 monks from the abbey of Citeaux in France travelled down Beaulieu River to the site just at the edge of the river to build their English domain, literally stone by stone.

Only two original buildings remain. The monks' refectory is now **Beaulieu Parish Church** (open to visitors) and the **Domus** is where the lay brothers, those who assisted the choir monks with manual tasks such as farming and building, lived. On the ground floor of the Domus, a dramatic video portrays the abbey's history alongside an exhibition describing the monks' daily lives.

A duck's eye view of the Beaulieu River

New Forest Activities The Old Forge, High St, Beaulieu SO42 7YA
ⓣ 01590 612377 ⓦ www.newforestactivities.co.uk.

It was raining lightly as I stepped into my kayak on the shores of the Beaulieu River. I was marginally enthused for this maritime adventure as heavier showers were predicted for later that day. Fortunately, however, New Forest Activities is well-stocked with wet-weather gear and I was given waterproof trousers along with my life preserver.

I was in a group of four. Steve, our instructor, patiently helped everyone get into their kayaks – even a slightly nervous man who couldn't swim and didn't even appear to like water much – and we began to paddle. Steve showed us how to twist the blade gently and how to use our torso for momentum so that we didn't get sore arms and we were off, literally skimming the water's surface to give us a duck's eye view.

As we rounded one of the sharp bends in this tranquil river, we spotted a little egret which looked especially brilliant white on that dark day and I realised that the rain has its benefits. This was a more subtle pleasure: the gentle water drops patting on the smooth river water, the muted pinky-purples of shrubs and trees and the distinct feeling that it was less about the kayaking than about being at one with the river.

Kayaks sit so low in the water that we could see how the saltflats rise up on top of mud piles. Behind them, the ancient oak woodland of the

Ironically, King John never witnessed the results of his good intentions because the buildings took 42 years to complete and he died before what would become the largest Cistercian abbey in England was finished. The land, already known as Bellus Locus Regis, meaning 'beautiful land of the king' in Latin, was then renamed Beaulieu by the French monks. Because the local Forest people didn't speak French, they pronounced Beau Lieu as 'Bewley', as it has been known ever since.

On the day I visited, Brother William, a costumed guide named Bill who plays his part and knows his history so well it's hard to believe he is not a real monk, was rushing through the cloisters, his simple sandals peeking out from beneath his brown robes that flowed behind him. He paused in his busy day to chat, something a real monk would not have had time to do.

eastern shore furnished a green backdrop and Steve explained that the juxtaposition of these two habitats is extremely rare. The monks from Beaulieu Abbey kept salt pans in the river to gather salt for the purpose of preserving food.

We inspected odd green shoots sprouting from the top of the flats and Steve told us that this is the now highly sought-after samphire which is the trendy 'freshly stemmed' plant that garnishes fish dishes in fancy restaurants. It is the first flowering plant to colonise new saltmarsh and sells for quite a bit on the open market. Don't even think about collecting it here in this highly guarded river, though. Lord Montagu protects his fishing rights that have been passed down since the monks' time as fiercely as they did.

We paddled upriver towards Beaulieu and had terrific views of the very expensive properties that line the eastern shore. This is a clever way to get further upriver where larger craft can't go except at very high tide. As with all things on the Beaulieu Estate, comings and goings are carefully scrutinised and Lord Montagu's harbourmaster keeps a close watch on every boat that comes in and out of the river. You can't launch a canoe or kayak here, let alone moor for a few hours, without paying a fee.

It's an easy paddle and experienced kayakers might be bored but it's an ideal way to see one of the few privately owned rivers in the world close up. As we landed back on shore, even the non-nautical participant said he enjoyed the trip.

'I would have awakened well before dawn to attend one of seven masses of the day,' Bill explained. 'I would have had one meal, usually a vegetable stew and a bit of bread. If I'd done especially fine work, I might earn an extra piece of cheese or an egg – a pittance.'

I smiled to realise this is where the expression 'earning your pittance' comes from. Meal times don't sound very exciting – Bill explained that the monks ate in silence except for one who stood in the pulpit and read from the Bible while the others ate.

As a choir monk, Brother William probably came from an educated family but unlike the lay brothers, he would have taken the strict vows of obedience, chastity and celibacy that were the foundation of the Cistercian order. Bill explained that being a monk was one of the safest jobs in the country because 'the king couldn't enlist you to fight in battles.' While many men became monks for religious reasons, others opted for this work because they received food and shelter in exchange for work and were, in effect, absolved from responsibilities of everyday life.

A man who became a monk might also bring status to a family if he became an abbot or prior, positions that might involve travel or even interactions with the king. Beaulieu was a relatively wealthy abbey in its time with further holdings in Oxfordshire, Berkshire and Devon. 'The abbot here was very senior and in good favour with the king,' explained Brother William. 'Perhaps it's because it was bestowed by kings.'

This is one of the few abbeys in England that offered permanent sanctuary, meaning that people in trouble with the law or just down on their luck, would be offered refuge here. 'The monks turned a blind eye as long as you behaved yourself inside these walls,' explained Bill. He chuckled as he dispelled misconceptions that people have about Beaulieu Abbey. 'People think that it always would have been quiet and sombre here but actually when the king came to visit, he brought an entourage of hundreds of people. There was excessive debauchery inside these walls at royal parties.'

Bill explained that the monks' fortunes rose and fell but that life on the whole was pretty good until the Reformation. When Henry VIII closed all the monasteries in England, he ordered all the buildings to be completely destroyed. The stone from Beaulieu was then used to construct the castles of Calshot, Hurst and Cowes on the Isle of Wight as defence points in case the French invaded. Monks became teachers or went to the continent but the closures were rough on local people.

'The Reformation had an enormous impact on Beaulieu townspeople as the closure of the Abbey left many people jobless,' explained Bill. 'Outside the walls of the abbey were businesses like tanneries and wood masons who serviced the needs of the abbey. And because the monks looked after the sick and disenfranchised, these people had nowhere to go when the abbey was destroyed.'

It's lucky that anything survives at all. By the **Clock House** and along **Mill Pond Walk**, portions of the 12-foot-high exterior wall that once surrounded the entire 58 acres of the abbey precinct still stand. (The Great Close was much larger, with about 8,500 acres incorporating the abbey's outposts.)

The precinct walls would have enclosed all of the abbey's main buildings, including stables, guesthouses, a saddler and blacksmith's forge. Shoes were a main industry of the abbey because each monk received two pairs of shoes each year; he was given more if engaged in heavy outdoor work.

The cloister now has an herb garden which grows plants the monks would have used for medicinal, veterinary and culinary purposes. As seen in the **cloister** today, they would have grown daffodil for antiseptic purposes, mint and thyme as digestive aids, lavender to cure 'pains of the head' and penny royal to alleviate toothache. But Bill explained that this would have been a place for quiet contemplation rather than a garden. Herbs would have been grown in several locations elsewhere within the precinct.

The abbey church

It would be easy to pass out of the abbey and miss the ruins behind the Domus, especially on a busy day. But it's only when you wander among the outlines in gravel of what was once the largest Cistercian church in England that you get a clear picture of this property's importance in British history.

An information board shows how the abbey church might have looked in the 1300s. There is also an audio tour, and accompanying text that can be downloaded from the website which makes a visit to the remains more meaningful.

The locations of the 68-foot-high marble columns that supported the roof have been marked out with rubble piles. As you walk down the centre aisle towards the high altar represented now by a box hedge, you begin to appreciate the scale of this immense structure. Oddly, few people seem to venture out here so you might find yourself alone with the birds for a moment of contemplation amid what can be a chaotically busy tourist attraction.

But don't stop there. Continue along the main road past the picnic area to where excavations in 1987–89 uncovered **Fulling Mill**. Once thought to be a wine press, this is where the monks improved cloth through beating, shrinking, thickening and cleaning.

Palace House

Most visitors head straight to the Motor Museum as this is the first stop after the ticket office. But if you want to see Palace House in relative quiet, it's best to go directly to the far end of the property. If you're

Enterprising monks or ruthless predators?

'Think of Beaulieu Abbey as the ancient Tesco or Walmart of its day,' said Richard Reeves, librarian at the New Forest Centre, with a twinkle in his eye. The image of monks living a pure life of prayer and helping the disenfranchised doesn't tell the whole story. Of course they did practise all those altruistic deeds but there also was an element of hardcore business about them. 'The monks gradually pushed the boundaries of their land and also helped themselves to the king's deer.' Richard explained that the monks allowed deer to wander onto their land but then devised traps in fencing that made it impossible for them to get back out. Although they were reprimanded for taking deer, the monks often had encroached land gifted to them, much to the annoyance of their neighbours.

The deer incident, as well as territorial disputes with neighbours, is recorded in the cartulary, the collection of records for the abbey. As the monks gradually began occupying land outside the official boundary between the Great Close and the king's forest, Edward II officially extended their enclosure for which the monks paid rent. But that didn't go down well with neighbours. In 1325, an organised demonstration of local residents destroyed the monks' boundary wall and led to considerable animosity between monks and locals.

But this type of behaviour wasn't so unusual at this time. Although the monks guarded their rights and territorial boundaries closely, the Forest had a history of encroachment generally. There was a long-held tradition that if someone could build a structure with a roof overnight and have a fire going by morning than he was the rightful owner. After that, legal action was required to get someone off the property.

Whether or not the monks were a dominant enterprise is open to interpretation. But they clearly had a keen business sense. The few records that remain show that the monks leased lands and operated a profitable enterprise, particularly with their wool production. The monks of Beaulieu Abbey were known for the high quality of their wool.

Although the Cistercian ideal was to achieve complete self-sufficiency, it is unrealistic to think the monks would have had all the manpower and skills they needed within their community. Records in late medieval times show that the monks leased lands, which gave them an income and a staff.

lucky, you'll tour the house in relative solitude and get a genuine feeling for what it was like to live here during the Victorian era.

To get to the house and abbey from the ticket office is about a ten-minute walk, or you can take the longest **monorail** in the country, a visually jarring gimmick to transport visitors from one end of the estate to the other. It is shamefully out of context but there is a nice view of the gardens from its elevated position. You can also ride a replica 1912 double-decker bus that goes back and forth from the abbey to the Motor Museum in summer. Be sure to walk through the gardens at least one way though, to properly appreciate this tranquil setting.

Today's visitors are invited to step back in time with museum guides dressed as Victorian-era staff. When I arrived, I was greeted by Barkham, a housemaid here in 1889. She told me she is addressed only by her surname but the head housekeeper would have been honoured with the title 'Mrs' in acknowledgement of her senior status.

Barkham had just finished dusting the stairs before the family awakened and she needed to get back downstairs. 'If a family member passes me in the house, I need to turn away and face my back to them as if I am not here,' she explained in a hushed tone, as she straightened her pinafore. 'It's hard work – I am up at 5.30am to clean the grates and lay fresh fires for the day. My day doesn't end until 10pm – later if there is a party. But I'm lucky to have this job.'

She explained that housemaid jobs were highly sought after by uneducated girls, often those who grew up in the country as children of agricultural workers, because they were likely to be better fed and looked after than in the family home. From about the age of 13, these girls would seek employment. 'We also have access to a doctor here which I never would have at home.'

Barkham and her fellow 'downstairs' staffers get one half-day off each week and are required to be in church on Sunday mornings for two hours. The rest of the time is spent cleaning, keeping the house warm and welcoming, and listening for bells in the kitchen that summon her upstairs. Her time off can be cancelled at any moment if she is needed by the family. When there are parties at nearby homes, such as Rhinefield House near Brockenhurst, she goes with the family to assist the staff there.

Palace House is far from the grandest English stately home but it is easy to imagine living here. In the dining room, pewter plates are laid on a table carved from a single elm tree, and a log fire burns in winter.

The current Montagu family still enjoys Christmas dinner here and at the side of the fireplace pencilled markings record the heights of Montagu children.

Downstairs in the kitchen, the servants' bell indicator shows how family members called for their staffers. The bells would continue ringing for a few minutes to ensure staffers knew which room to go to. A menu printed on the kitchen blackboard changes daily to show what the family and staff might have eaten on that day in 1889.

Edward, the 3rd Baron Montagu of Beaulieu, and member of the House of Lords, inherited Beaulieu in 1951 at the age of 25 from his father, John. Due to high running costs, Edward decided to open parts of the house to the public at that time. He also placed five cars from the family collection in the entrance hall as a tribute to his father, a motoring enthusiast. This was the humble start of the Motor Museum.

Lord Montagu's written recollections of growing up at Palace House appear throughout, making a visit feel like an intimate tour. He still lives in portions of the house and for an extra fee you can arrange a private tour of his apartments when the family is not in residence. The most likely times are Tuesday to Thursday in the spring but it's best to call ahead to be sure tours are running.

Palace House has been a Montagu family home since 1538, when Henry VIII's dissolution of the monasteries was completed. Lord Montagu's ancestor, Sir Thomas Wriothesley, later 1st earl of Southampton, purchased the property that had belonged to Beaulieu Abbey from the king. With the purchase came full monastic rights which Lord Beaulieu exercises today. Sir Thomas viewed the property more as a source of income than a home but he chose the former Cistercian monastery's 14th-century gatehouse for accommodation and used it as a hunting lodge.

In the 19th century, Lord Montagu's grandfather, Lord Henry Scott, expanded the building to become a family residence. From the front garden, the difference in the stone used in medieval times and that of the Victorian addition is apparent. The Clock House, one of the only remaining Abbey buildings, is where monks administered aid to the poor who knocked on the outer gates.

People who were offered sanctuary continued to the Great Gatehouse which is now Palace House. The current private dining room and drawing room upstairs were once chapels used by non-monastic guests who wouldn't have been allowed to worship in the abbey church.

Palace House gardens

The gardens are especially lovely in spring when some 15 species of daffodils carpet the moat and lawn outside the house. Further towards the exit, a **Victorian garden** is in the process of being recreated. In the **kitchen garden**, a glass house which Henry, the 1st Lord Montagu built, contains a vine from that time.

During school holidays, organised activities take place on the lawn by the mill pond, including Easter egg hunts, face painting and Victorian games like skittles. An aproned housemaid, dipping from Victorian character to present-day staffer, told me: 'It's wonderful to see that children are captivated by these simple garden games when they spend so much time on computers and electronic games. They love the simplicity of tossing a ring over a pole and knocking down wooden pegs.'

On the day I visited, children raced around the lawn and the woman in a long black dress could easily have been a Victorian nanny. In the large open space between the house and Motor Museum, there are distinctly non-Victorian activities during school holidays for an extra charge, including go-kart rides and assault courses. There is enough to do here with children to make it a really full day, especially during the holidays.

A self-service restaurant near the entrance to the attraction has a few outdoor tables but on a sunny day it's better to bring a picnic and enjoy the gardens. Of several picnic areas, the nicest is just off the main pathway from the house inside a large square garden boxed in by hedges and trees. On the main road by the church ruins, a large picnic area has picnic tables and an enclosure useful for rainy days.

Beaulieu Motor Museum

I knew that the Motor Museum boasts a world-class collection of cars but it wasn't until I chatted with some of the knowledgeable staff that I saw the museum as a fascinating chronicle of motoring history, they helped me stop and think about how the automobile revolutionised the world.

Much of the museum is staffed by volunteers who are either stationed at the information desk or wandering among visitors. They give guided tours throughout the day which will enhance your visit immensely, whether you are a car enthusiast or not. I stopped to chat with volunteer John Ellis and found myself whisked into a whirl of entertaining facts about cars and the important contributions of John, 2nd Lord Montagu of Beaulieu, to the motoring industry.

John showed me some of the collection's highlights like the **1899 Daimler** in which John Montagu took the Prince of Wales (later Edward VII) for a drive, thereby cementing their friendship but also forging the connection between Daimler and the Royal Family. Apparently the Prince of Wales had so much fun that he ordered a similar car for himself, much to the chagrin of his minders.

It was also in this car that Lord Montagu, the MP for the New Forest, drove from Beaulieu to the Palace of Westminster, making this the first car to drive into the House of Commons Yard. 'The speed limit at that time was 12 miles per hour,' John explained with a chuckle. 'But Lord Montagu wanted to make a point so he drove faster than that as part of his campaign to raise awareness of the importance of motoring to improving society. In 1903 he helped pass a bill that raised the speed limit to 20 miles per hour and required all drivers to display registered number plates.'

John Montagu was a forward thinker who campaigned to improve Britain's roads after World War I. 'He believed that motor cars would bring greater political, economic and social changes than the railways,' said John Ellis. John, 2nd Lord Montagu, campaigned for elevated roadways and for a motorway that would link London with Liverpool. He didn't live to see this dream to fruition because the first motorway was not built until 1958. He was also an early supporter of the Channel Tunnel. 'He was so much more than a rich guy with a penchant to drive fast,' said John Ellis. 'He started the first car magazine, *The Car Illustrated,* he instigated the law that raised the speed limit in the UK and he was a founding member of the RAC.'

Be sure not to miss the **1909 Rolls Royce Silver Ghost** (registration number R1909) which was John Montagu's pride and joy and is

A jumble of transport

The Motor Museum hosts numerous events throughout the year, including the International Autojumble in the autumn, which is the largest event of its kind in Europe. The summer Boatjumble and a smaller Autojumble in spring attract many enthusiasts, as does a motorcycle ride-in day in July and fireworks in October.

pictured in the portrait at the top of the stairs in Palace House. You might not realise that this car was reconstructed from a breakdown truck in Berwick-on-Tweed in Northumberland. 'The chassis was in excellent condition, so it just needed to be redesigned to make a stunning vehicle,' explained John Ellis. Ask a staffer to see the photo that shows it in its original condition.

When we surveyed the monstrosity that is the steam-operated **1880 Grenville**, I had to laugh at how far car design has progressed. 'We still take this out,' John told me, 'but it takes two hours to fire it up and three people to operate it.' It is believed to be the oldest self-propelled, passenger-carrying road vehicle that still works. There is a lot of just plain fun here, too. Cars used for advertising, like the butterball design of the Outspan Orange are a treat to examine close-up. The original Chitty Chitty Bang Bang is here, as well as many famous racing cars and some land-speed record-breakers.

An excursion into falconry

I was nervous but I didn't want to admit it. I signed up for an introductory session in falconry with Paul Manning, an experienced falconer and accredited trainer, based at the Countryside Education Trust's Out of Town Centre in Beaulieu. In summer, Paul and his birds can be found in the cloister at Beaulieu Abbey for flight demonstrations.

That day, Paul's falcons, hawks and one very large owl, sat patiently on their perches waiting for the session to begin. As I eyed the birds, some with steely gazes, I wondered, what had made me think I wanted to do this?

When Paul told my group that in just a few hours, one of the hawks would fly straight at us from a tree to retrieve food from our hands, my stomach dropped. But he was so eminently confident in each of us, including the 12-year-old boy on my course, that I gradually relaxed.

Paul is not keen on hotel-style afternoons of falconry in which patrons hold birds for a few minutes and then head off for afternoon tea. Instead he demands that participants on his course understand the discipline behind falconry. So the three-and-a-half-hour session began with a talk from Paul in which he described the evolution of falconry from an essential hunting technique thousands of years ago, to the rise of birds as a status symbol in the 1500s, to the sport's gradual decline with the advent of guns and over-hunting of birds of prey.

As fascinating as Paul's speech about the history of falconry was (and it really was), I couldn't help but focus on the peregrine falcon beside him who, as if to taunt me, occasionally let out a rather loud squawk. Gradually, though, I was drawn in by Paul's obvious passion and expansive knowledge.

He explained how his interest began. 'When I was 13, a hawk escaped from London Zoo and began to attack little dogs in Regent's Park. I was mesmerised from that day.' Paul works regularly with young offenders and believes that the responsibility required to handle birds can make troubled youngsters see life differently. 'Falconry teaches humility because you have to serve the bird. It is life-enhancing to be around such an indomitable spirit.'

Each participant was given his or her own bird to look after for the session so that we experienced some responsibility and a brief bonding. When Paul handed me my own small falcon, I was moved by the dedication of this ex-rugby player and native Londoner who maintains an ancient tradition. He described how he's trained each of his birds, beginning with sitting motionless for hours in a room while the bird learns to trust him. Then the endless days of gradual steps, to the time of letting the bird fly free and knowing it will return. This is not a job from which you can take a day off or you lose the trust of your birds. Worryingly for us, if we jerked away or dropped the food when the bird flew towards us, we could ruin all of Paul's hard work in one afternoon.

Hence my anxiety when a few hours later I stood in a field watching Belle, a Harris Hawk with piercing eyes, poised on a tree limb, waiting for my signal to approach. Paul handed me a piece of food and told me to hide it quickly. As I tucked my hand behind my back, I could have sworn that I was holding a chicken foot.

I forgot about my squeamishness in the next few moments, though, as I stood poised with arm outstretched. Belle swooped from a resting point across the field and in one magical dive, landed like a breath of air on my fist. She gobbled down the food before I even realised it was gone from my hand. When Paul handed me the next course – a larger piece of baby chick with fluff intact, I realised that, yes indeed, the appetiser had been a chicken foot.

By the end of the afternoon, I was handling chicken guts (albeit with my thick glove) and walking comfortably with Inajah, a lanner falcon, poised on my arm. Although I am not comfortable with hunting as an activity, I can see how a hunting expedition with Paul and his birds of prey would be exhilarating and timeless. But it's enough for me that here in the ancient woods of the New Forest, I've practised an art that hasn't changed in a thousand years.

Birdwatching at Beaulieu

For information on birdwatching and other nature events in the New Forest:
Countryside Education Trust ⓣ 01590 612401 ⓦ www.cet.org.uk.

I am not a birdwatcher, but I joined a dedicated group of them and their intrepid leader, Graham Giddens, for a dawn chorus with nightingales that I saw advertised on the website of the Countryside Education Trust. As I drove to the Needs Ore Reserve at 05.15, a private reserve on the Beaulieu Estate, I was treated to a glimpse of the forest awakening. Rabbits scampered from the middle of the road and along the B3045, a normally busy thoroughfare, there were no cars, only ponies munching roadside grass. So I was ready to mingle with nature when I arrived at the meeting point from where Graham, an experienced ornithologist who runs birdwatching holidays, escorted me to the reserve.

Our group of eight began by searching for a nightingale, which Graham had heard in the gorse bushes while he waited for us. My more experienced classmates were captivated but I couldn't distinguish the nightingale's song. I moved closer to Graham and leaned forward slightly, feeling sure this would improve my hearing capabilities. I strained to block out the geese who blasted their morning trumpets and then for a brief moment all went quiet and the nightingale treated us to a lengthy chorus. So this is what all the poems are about – I heard it then, loud and clear, unmistakable.

Graham explained that the nightingale population has dropped here owing to the profusion of roe deer which graze away the scrub. Robins then come in and nest and when the nightingales return from Africa each year, the robins chase them away. But efforts have begun to remove deer, and the nightingales are slowly returning.

Graham darted from bush to bush, pointing out birds and their calls. 'Boo doo, boo doo,' he imitated. 'Can you hear it?' Then he bounded off in the direction of another bush, folding his tripod in one smooth motion, almost as if it was a third arm, and set it back down so we all could have a view of the next sighting, a whitethroat warbler. Suddenly Graham jumped up, pointing at the sky. In an oddly muted exclamation of excitement, he called, 'Display flight! Display flight!' A bird swooped and dove above us – I was not sure what type but whatever it was, it was showing off to the lady of his species. As we moved on, Graham smiled. 'Top spotting here,' he said, and then he darted off down a narrow path, tripod tucked up at his side, through tall hedging. We followed behind in a straight line as if we were his ducklings. We emerged on to an open field where Graham pointed out a large group of swallows sitting on fences and gathered in an oak tree. 'They are resting after flying from France to come here to mate. They will have been flying against the wind and are exhausted now.'

We stopped to observe a bar-tailed godwit (a sighting that pleased Graham) and then crossed the field to a hide where we all were grateful for a few minutes of relative warmth on this unseasonably chilly May morning. Graham passed around a packet of biscuits and then we had our big treat of the day. We had been watching avocets – a type of wader that has been absent in this area until the past two years and now is returning in great numbers thanks to the work to improve habitats on the Beaulieu Estate – when two floated just in front of the hide and Graham told us that the male was showing off for the female. I focused my binoculars on the pair and suddenly he was on top of her and for a very quick moment we witnessed this not-so-private act.

I am glad to have attended the session because it encouraged me to think more about the world going on around me while I go about my daily life. I slowed down that morning, listening to and watching life on the marshes. I was surprised by how thrilling it felt to spot an unusual bird, most likely because Graham's passion and knowledge are infectious. I'm struck by how many species fly to my little corner of the world every year from Africa and the Mediterranean, navigating by the stars to reach this tiny stretch of Hampshire coast, where until now I had rushed past, oblivious.

The Out of Town Centre

Palace Lane, SO42 7YG ℗ 01590 612401 ⓦ www.cet.org.uk.

The Beaulieu Estate is also home to the Countryside Education Trust (CET), a charity started in 1975 by Lord Montagu and the broadcaster, Jack Hargreaves. About 1,000 schoolchildren annually visit the Trust's Out of Town Centre to take part in residential programmes that are designed to 'connect children with the countryside'. Children work with animals and vegetables on the centre's farm in the morning and evenings and do nature coursework during the day. They also visit the centre's extraordinary treehouse, a self-sufficient building that operates with solar panels and recycled rainwater and has a spiral staircase that leads up among the treetops.

'As a nation, we have become divorced from the countryside,' David Bridges, director of the centre, told me as we toured the small campus of buildings and farmland. 'We drive past fields but have no connection to them or understanding of how it all works. People assume that everything in the New Forest is wild, like the animals they see roaming but in fact it is a highly managed environment.'

That message is not just directed at the schoolchildren who stay here. The CET hosts many community programmes that are bookable on their website, including falconry, birdwatching, parent and toddler groups, forage and feast classes, bee-keeping and open days – all designed to foster a deeper understanding of the natural world. Self-catering weekends for groups of friends or a family can be arranged.

I've done quite a few programmes sponsored by the CET and always have emerged enriched and inspired – just what the organisation hopes to achieve. 'When people visit here, I'd like to think they take away a sense of awe, together with a practical understanding of how the countryside works.'

Food and drink

Steff's Kitchen Fairweather's Garden Centre, High St SO42 7YB ☏ 01590 612307. This café in the back of Fairweather's is a pleasant spot for lunch or tea especially in warm weather. The outdoor terrace, always open, overlooks the nursery.

⑧ Hatchet Pond

Although a relatively small pond, this is the largest body of water in the New Forest, and generally a busy place. Ponies and cattle come to drink, donkeys arrive in hopes of raiding tourists' picnics, and photographers head here at sunset to capture the outlines of trees against the often brilliant purples and pinks that paint the sky behind Beaulieu Heath.

Even on the bleakest days, there is likely to be at least one tent containing at least one fisherman determined to capture carp – the record is reportedly a 31-pounder -- and also bream, pike, eels and roach. The pond, just outside East Boldre at the junction of the B3054 and the B3055, was created in the 18th century to provide power for an iron mill. You need to have a fishing permit from the Forestry

Commission and an Environment Agency rod licence (which can be purchased online).

Forestry Commission permits can be bought at East Boldre post office just by Hatchet Pond or the nearby Roundhill Campsite in Brockenhurst, and season tickets are available from the Forestry Commission's headquarters in Queen's House in Lyndhurst.

Beaulieu Organic Farmshop
Hatchet SO42 7WA ℗ 01590 612666.

'It's nice to know we provide quality stuff,' said butcher Les Bowden as he hoisted a chunk of meat on to the counter and began to slice. He smiled broadly and I could only smile back.

Beaulieu Organic Farmshop, located on Hatchet Lane (B3054) between Hatchet Pond and Beaulieu village, opened when the much-loved Warborne Organic Farm in Boldre closed its farm shop in 2010. Les and John Jordan, Warborne's former butchers, decided there was enough demand for organic meat and produce that they could have their own shop.

On any given day, a group of people gather in the small shop and chat as they select organic vegetables, baked goods and, of course, meats from behind the counter where John and Les preside. Chatter ranges from Forest gossip to the state of the economy but it's always friendly and it's always fun. People don't mind waiting here because it's a place where buying food recalls a time when food shopping was as much about forging community ties as it was about stocking the larder.

'People are fed up with supermarkets,' said John. 'They're beginning to realise that mass-produced vegetables and meat have no flavour so it's not worth that bit of savings.'

Les agrees that more people are thinking carefully about what they eat and avoiding chemicals and other additives. 'Organic is a choice – it's really a lifestyle choice – and we get customers from all over the area and beyond who don't mind paying a bit extra for more flavour, as well as the assurance of no preservatives or added colours.'

John and Les hang their beef for 21 days to allow it to mature. 'Supermarkets are likely to kill it one day and pack it the next,' explained John, with a slight shudder. 'The meat changes colour as soon as you open the pack,' he sighed, shaking his head. He said that some people who come in are bothered by the look of dirt-encrusted carrots but that most shoppers know that translates to ultra-fresh, flavour-packed vegetables.

'We try to source everything as locally as possible but the Forest is a forest, not farming country,' explained Les. That's why there is European produce on the shelves in winter but once growing season begins in England, John and Les turn to local farms for fruit and veg.

In that respect, running a local, organic farm shop here in non-farming country is more of a challenge than it might seem. But as Les pointed out, 'buying local is in vogue.'

⑨ Beaulieu Heath

If you're standing near Beaulieu Heath and hear a distant whine, look up, because it's likely to be a model aircraft. Beaulieu Heath played a part in World War II when a three-runway airfield was built here, the remnants of which can still be seen. The largest block is used for model aircraft flying and smaller flying strips now serve as bike paths. To fly a model plane here, you need to join the **British Model Flying Association** (BMFA) for proper insurance coverage and to obtain an annual flying permit. Contact Bryan Targett of the Beaulieu Model Flying Committee (*023 8089 1464*).

This is a sometimes eerie place to explore. Aside from the fierce winds that take hold here, the open heath makes exhilarating cycling terrain. Ponies and cattle wander freely amid the scrub and there are views of the Isle of Wight.

⑩ East Boldre

East Boldre is an intriguing place, defying the traditional English village that develops around a church and town hall. Like many other New Forest settlements, it is a linear development, about two miles long and only a quarter of a mile wide, without a true centre. It began as workers' settlements along the western boundary of the Beaulieu Estate and was originally known as 'Beaulieu Rails', in reference to the wooden railings that topped the earth bank marking that boundary.

This is one of the best places to see an **encroachment community**, which this area is known for, when squatters hastily erected dwellings before the authorities could be bothered to enact legal proceedings of eviction. Although there are now many modern homes, you can still see some old thatched and cob cottages. Workers from Buckler's Hard and nearby farms, as well as from the iron works in Sowley and brickworks at Bailey's Hard, took up residence here on what was Crown land.

This arrangement would have benefitted employers of Beaulieu because in the 18th and early 19th centuries, each parish was responsible for its 'poor parishioners'. So to have employees living outside the parish meant that the Beaulieu employers were responsible only for these workers' wages, not the poor tax levied by the parish. Boldre parish wasn't necessarily happy about these encroachments but did not have the authority to evict them. The hamlet at Beaulieu Rails ultimately led to disputes between the parishes of Beaulieu and Boldre.

East Boldre has an impressive **aviation history**. The fifth flying school in the world opened here in 1910 with an airfield at East Boldre. William McArdle and American, J Armstrong-Drexel built two sheds and a rough runway, despite being refused permission by the then Office of Woods. Just two years later, the school closed. But in 1915, the Royal Flying Corps (predecessor of the RAF) established a training school for pilots here called RFC Beaulieu. The present-day village hall was the officers' mess.

The Beaulieu letters

Evidence of aviation history can be seen today in the form of letters spelling 'Beaulieu' which were carved into the heath sometime between 1910 and 1916. The Beaulieu letters were covered during World War II and gradually became overgrown with vegetation. An enthusiastic group of volunteers recently exposed them and restored them to their chalky white glory.

The letters are 15 feet high, making the whole word extend for 110 feet. Debate continues as to their origin but according to Henry Cole, a Forestry Commission volunteer ranger who was involved with their most recent restoration, they served as a turning point for the 1910 Bournemouth Air Show, during which pilots had to fly around a large wooden tower. Henry also suggests that it might have been a practical joke that Drexel played on McArdle after the latter got lost on his way back from the show and landed in Fordingbridge.

They're obviously best seen from the air, but you can walk right up to them if you're willing to do a bit of sleuthing. If it has been raining, the ground will be wet – wellies are best. Park at Hatchet Pond car park and cross the road (B3054). At the small arrow sign pointing to the car park, walk straight ahead for 15 yards. You will see a narrow diagonal path. Walk half right for 60 yards at which point you will see a clearing in the gorse bushes off to the right. There is no direct path so you'll need to pick your way through the gorse for 40 yards to the clearing where you will be rewarded with a giant 'Beaulieu' inscription. Great fun.

Food and drink

Turfcutter's Arms Main Rd, SO42 7WL ⓣ 01590 612331 ⓦ www.theturfcutters.co.uk. This isn't the best food in the Forest but this old-fashioned pub is well-situated if you're out walking, fishing or cycling and need sustenance. The plain wood floorboards and wall hangings of horses and riders are a welcome change from the slick décor of modern gastro pubs. At lunchtime, dogs sprawl beneath tables and hungry walkers tuck into their ploughman's. The standard pub fare is decent and the atmosphere is jolly with a lot of local flavour; one small room off the main area has a warm fire. The large garden with plenty of tables is ideal for families with small children or just a pleasant spot to enjoy lunch.

⑪ St Leonard's Grange

The imposing ruins of St Leonard's Grange on a small, rural road about half a mile from Buckler's Hard are all that is left of what was once the largest barn, or grangia, at one of Beaulieu Abbey's farming outposts. It stands at the edge of the road, seemingly forgotten, with birds nesting in the medieval windows. If you look closely, you'll notice the bizarre barn within a barn which dates from the 16th century when farmers used materials from the crumbling monastic structure to build a second barn within it.

Granges were managed by conversi, or lay brothers, a kind of 'monks' assistants', who attended far fewer services and carried out practical tasks. This enabled the choir monks to devote themselves to prayer, meditation and ministering to the poor. The lay brothers worked the land and sent grain and other produce to the abbey. The abbey in turn sent back bread, fish, salt and ever-important beer.

Monks at the nearby holding of Bergerie handled the sheep and wool production for which Beaulieu Abbey was renowned. Wool produced at Bergerie was sent to the abbey's wool store in Southampton and exported to the continent, bringing the monks a generous profit.

A bench on the opposite side of the road facing the remains of what must have been a massive building makes the ideal spot to have a rest and contemplate the world of the monks.

Food and drink

East End Arms East End SO41 5SY ⓣ 01590 626223 ⓦ www.eastend
arms.co.uk. Dire Straits fans probably already know that John Illsley, the
band's bass guitarist, owns this old-time pub in this very quiet corner
of Hampshire. It's been getting progressively more slick as the years go
by and is less pubby in the dining room than it used to be but the bar
still feels like a village watering hole. Ideal Sunday lunch spot but be
forewarned: it's hugely popular. It also has accommodation (see
page 93).

⑫ Buckler's Hard

ⓣ 01590 616203 ⓦ www.bucklershard.co.uk. The admission price covers
the village, Maritime Museum and Buckler's Hard Story, and car parking.

This tiny former port is overflowing with history from its inception in
the 1720s to its heyday as a shipbuilding centre in the late 18th and
early 19th centuries and through to its important role in preparations
for World War II invasions. Buckler's Hard was built with two rows of
workers' cottages lining the broad 'hard' that led down to the river, and
this view is remarkably unchanged. Eventually houses were built off the
main street, including Slab Row, so-called because the bark hadn't even
been taken off the wood used to construct the buildings. They were
demolished in the mid 19th century as the shipbuilding era came to an
end and the population declined.

The hamlet originated in the early 18th century when John, 2nd Duke
of Montagu, then owner of the Beaulieu Estate, envisioned the site as
Montagu Town, a free port for the import and export of sugar from
the West Indies. The Duke organised an expensive and well-equipped
expedition of seven ships to St Lucia, only to discover that the French
had the same idea and were well-entrenched by the time the English
got there. That changed the fate of the Duke's peaceful hamlet forever.

The name, which originally was 'Buckle's Hard', most likely derives
from a local family, the Buckles, who had lived there for generations and
used the site as a landing point for their boats. 'Hard' is the south coast
term to describe a landing point in a river where the banks are especially
soft. All you have to do is take the riverside walk from Beaulieu to see
just how soft.

This is an ideal location for shipbuilding, not only because the gravel
soil extends all the way down to the low-water mark but because of the
abundance of surrounding trees. In 1744, the Navy Board sent Henry

Adams to Buckler's Hard to supervise the building of the *Surprise*, the second ship to be built in the area. The first was the *Salisbury*, which was actually constructed further upriver just outside of Beaulieu village.

The Shipwright's Cottage and the Maritime Museum

'It's an accident of history that Buckler's Hard became a shipbuilding centre,' said museum staffer, Eileen Sprat, one of the Living History guides at Buckler's Hard. 'It's only because the French beat us to the sugar trade that the village took on its role.' Eileen, a New Forest resident and former teacher, poses as a shipwright's wife during summer and school holidays. She can be found sporting her long skirt, prim blouse and cap in the **Shipwright's Cottage** on the West Terrace or wandering through the hamlet. During her many years working at Buckler's Hard, she has studied the village's history carefully.

Eileen credited Henry Adams with having the savvy and contacts to make Buckler's Hard such an important shipbuilding centre. 'I believe Henry Adams was successful because he anticipated what the Navy needed. And he had the right contacts in the Navy to ensure he got the contracts.'

She and other Living History guides are full of interesting tales that show visitors how life might have been here in the 19th century. Eileen shared an anecdote about the expression 'your number's up' which she believes originates from Henry Adams. 'Each of Adams's workers had a number. If Adams wasn't satisfied with that worker's productivity, he would hang the number from a prominent hook to inform the worker that either he wasn't going to get paid or in the worst case scenario, he would be fired which meant he'd lose his home.'

The **Maritime Museum and the Buckler's Hard Story** seems small but it is packed with information that illustrates the breadth of historical roles played out here. This was the centre of shipbuilding during the Battle of Trafalgar and staffers have a strong sense of pride that Admiral Nelson's favourite ship, *Agamemnon*, was launched here. Buckler's Hard became a hub of wartime efforts again during World War II and the video describing this area's role is well worth watching. The Beaulieu River was a busy place as segments of 'Mulberry Harbours', the temporary concrete harbours used to offload cargo at Normandy, were constructed here. There also are exhibits dedicated to local sailors, including Sir Francis Chichester, who trialled his yacht, *Gipsy Moth IV*, in the Beaulieu River and the Solent before sailing it around the world.

During recent renovations when a pew was moved in the chapel in order to install a new floor, workers noticed a void under the altar. Further investigations revealed a cellar containing broken wine and brandy bottles. Because it is known that the chapel was once a residential cottage, local experts believe that this may have been a hub of smuggling. 'Although we can't say for sure that it went on, it certainly seems plausible that goods may have been hidden here after being brought down the Beaulieu River from the Solent,' said Jane

Living in history

As you wander along the sloping main street of Buckler's Hard, it's tempting to daydream about what it might be like to live here. The 18th-century cottages built originally as part of a free port for the importing and exporting of sugar, and later inhabited by shipbuilders, are now used by the Maritime Museum and the Master Builder's Hotel. Others are rented from the Beaulieu Estate by private tenants. Jane Mills, Manager of the Buckler's Hard visitor attraction, lives in a cottage owned by the estate just behind the main street. So what's it like having your home in a village that is essentially a living museum?

'It's magical, when the visitors leave and the gates are locked, we return to our own very special small community of ten full-time residents,' Jane told me as we meandered down the central path, virtually devoid of visitors on an early spring day. 'Christmas Day, the only day the museum isn't open, is probably the most precious time, especially if there has been snow. The lights of the Christmas tree in the village twinkle, and the hotel guests and village residents have the whole place to themselves.'

She clearly appreciates living in a place that embodies so much history as well as the possibility of more. 'It's incredible that such a small place has played such a big part in England's history. It's impossible not to think about all that's gone on here and the people who might have lived in my cottage long before me.'

Jane told me that past staff and their families who have lived in the cottage insist that they've heard thumps in the attic and seen apparitions, particularly a worried child in 18th-century clothing. Jane has heard unidentifiable sounds but won't go so far as to acknowledge sharing her home with ghosts. 'Who knows? With all that's gone on here before my time, I wouldn't rule out anything.'

Mills, Manager of Buckler's Hard. 'Historians have long speculated that smugglers brought liquor to inns at Buckler's Hard, and this could have been a hiding place.' The cellar and some of the findings are visible through a glass plate in the floor.

~~~><><~~~

Food and drink

Master Builder's Hotel SO42 7XB ℗ 01590 616253
Ⓦ www.themasterbuilders.co.uk. As well as being a pleasantly located place to stay (see page 94) this hotel has a pubby bar with lots of beams, long tables and a log fire, and a choice of bar food on offer. On warmer days, the lawn makes a perfect spot to watch boats on the river.

A cruise on the Beaulieu River

At the bottom of the hill, on the left of Buckler's Hard, a small cruise boat docks for a 30-minute tour downriver towards the Solent. The river is unusual for two reasons: it is one of the only privately owned rivers in the world and it has a double tide, which means that the tide goes out very slowly and comes in very quickly so that in essence, they overlap for a bit.

The inexpensive cruise is an ideal way to see much of the river's highlights. It takes you past opulent riverside houses that were requisitioned during World War II as bases for training spies, and you glimpse Gins, where the monks of Beaulieu kept their fishing boats. On the eastern shore are Exbury Gardens and you get close-up views of the saltmarshes and assortment of craft moored in the river. The guided tour points out the hand-dug oyster beds put in by the current Lord Montagu's grandfather. Oysters now grow wild here and Beaulieu is one of the few rivers clean enough to be licensed to harvest oysters. You'll also hear about salt production in the Beaulieu River and a few tales from World War II.

One of the best views is of the ancient barn at St Leonard's. Just as the boat begins to turn back towards Buckler's Hard, look around to see the tip of the triangle in the distance that forms the last remaining wall of this monastic ruin.

Note that if you only want to take the boat trip, you still need to pay an admission fee to Buckler's Hard. This is to stop people parking in the car park if they're not visiting the museum. If you're walking, enter the village through the public walking gate at the top of the Hard and you may take the boat without visiting any of the attractions; if you try to park in the car park without purchasing a ticket, you risk getting your vehicle clamped. You can also just walk from Beaulieu village (see below), take a boat ride and walk back.

Beaulieu Riverside Walk

At the bottom of the hill near the Buckler's Hard Marina is the beginning of the Riverside Walk to the village of Beaulieu. The two-mile trail is part of the Solent Way. There are two routes: a straight path through the forest or one that diverts to follow the edge of the river. Either provides a very different walk and it's worth taking one up and one back.

On the **riverside walk**, just past the marina at Keeping Marsh, is **a hide** for observing the many species of birds that live here during different times of the year. This wildlife site developed when dredgings from building the marina were put here and birds flocked to the site. Work is underway to prevent the wetland from naturally converting back to woodland. The walk continues along the riverbank and can be muddy at times although there are wooden walkways across the marshiest bits. Just before you reach the fields that ultimately lead to Beaulieu village, you can see a house with a tall chimney that was once part of the estate brickworks. This is where the *Salisbury*, the first ship to be built at Buckler's Hard was constructed.

The **path through the woods** makes a very pleasant contrast. Tall conifers line one side of the trail and on the other you catch glimpses of the river. I've walked here and found myself very close to deer without even breaking stride. They tend to eye walkers warily but stand still and watch people pass. Both paths have information boards describing the surroundings.

Southampton Coast: Exbury, Lepe and Eling

The coastal land east of the mouth of the Beaulieu River is not part of the New Forest (although it is part of the national park) and is distinctly different in character and landscape. When I first came to this area, I avoided the stony beach here despite a great love for the seashore, because of its proximity to urban Southampton, Fawley Power Station and the adjacent oil refinery.

How wrong I was. Although this coastline can't be compared to the glories of Dorset or Devon, or even further along the Hampshire coast, it has its own appeal, not least because it is so close to urban sprawl. One day after visiting **Calshot Castle**, I walked on the rocky beach of **Calshot Spit** and discovered that if you face south out to sea and keep the towers of the power station and oil refinery at your back, you are rewarded with fine views of the Solent and the excitement of watching the very busy shipping activity of Southampton Water.

I also was unaware, as I think many are, of the important nature reserves tucked in behind the coast here. **Calshot Marshes**, although small, attracts rare waterfowl. At **Lepe Country Park**, special habitats have been created to entice insects and birds. The most rewarding **cycling** is the off-road trail within the park but coming from Beaulieu, it is only accessible from main roads. Once at Lepe, though, you have the choice of several quiet lanes.

As you trudge along the bumpy shingle beach at Lepe and brace yourself against the inevitable wind, it's easy to imagine all the defence preparations made here from the time of Henry VIII right through to 1945. Remnants of World War II demonstrate this area's importance in the lead-up to D-day.

The urban nature reserves at **Testwood** are rewarding in a similar way to the experience at Calshot. The juxtaposition of suburban sprawl outside the gates makes the intricacies of nature more distinctive.

Few people realise that the New Forest extends to the shore at **Eling**. The village is very different in feel to the Forest but the coastal grazing on nearby marshes is a reminder of where you are. In any case, spending a morning at the tidal mill and walking through the surrounding marshes is so delightfully Slow and historic that it fits in well.

⑬ Exbury Gardens

Exbury O45 1AZ ⓣ 023 8089 1203 ⓦ www.exbury.co.uk. Guided walks with head gardener and other members of staff throughout the year. Closed Nov–Mar.

The New Forest isn't particularly noted for its grand gardens but Exbury, located just outside the Forest boundaries (but within the national park) enables this area to hold its own in the company of great gardens of England.

'The first thing you notice about Exbury is its scale,' said John Anderson, Exbury's head gardener. 'The contrast here is astounding, from the exotic colours of the azaleas and rhododendrons to the subtleties of rushes on a river walk. It's a huge challenge to maintain a garden that exists on so many levels: formal and wild areas, cascades, ponds and rock gardens.' I see what he means. In one short morning, I wandered through the highly manicured **Sundial Garden** over to the carefree **daffodil meadow** where the nodding yellow blossoms carpeted the field before a backdrop of the Beaulieu River.

I joined John on one of Exbury's guided tours which had been billed as a walk to view the early spring blooms of primroses and camellias but turned out to be so much more. Our small group of keen gardeners and dogs learned about the history of the house and titbits about the Rothschild family. Most interestingly, we discussed the evolution of the garden, from its incarnation as an arboretum when the Mitford family owned the estate, to its development as the largest rock garden in Europe according to the vision of Lionel de Rothschild and later his son Edmund.

John told us how even established gardens like this one are not static but constantly changing due to climate conditions, disease and overgrowth of shrubs. I began to feel less guilty about a mature shrub I'd removed from my own garden when I learned that John and his team sometimes remove large rhododendrons when they begin to crowd out smaller plants. 'The nice thing is that gardeners around England are now working as a team. We can find someone to take a plant if we can't use it here anymore.'

Exbury is known as a spring garden because of its celebrated collection of camellias, rhododendrons and azaleas, which peak in April and May. Roughly 70% of the 120,000 annual visitors come between mid-April and May, with another surge in October. Exbury has been voted one of the top ten sites for autumn colour in the UK by Visit England thanks to its waterside maples and prolific dogwoods.

There is no question that the flamboyant pinks, reds, oranges and yellows that flourish here in April are magnificent but there is something to be said for visiting Exbury off-season. In the absence of dramatic showpieces and hordes of visitors, it's easier to appreciate the garden as a whole.

John agreed: 'Personally I like the garden best in early spring before it goes over the top. When colours are more subtle, you are more aware of the garden as a whole. You also have the anticipation of what is to come. There are no blooms that have gone past their prime, only the early blossoms and the promise of those to follow.' Indeed. Without the crowds, I am more aware of the woodpeckers and birds and without the bright blossoms I notice how the paths are arranged and marvel at the foresight of Lionel Rothschild when he laid out his garden more than 90 years ago.

'I think about Lionel and his vision every day,' said John as we surveyed the **Azalea Bowl** from the Stone Bridge. 'It's extraordinary that he created a garden on this scale in just 20 years. And it's equally amazing that when his son Edmund inherited it he was able to interpret what his father had been doing and carry it forward despite the hardships of war years and this not being his primary home.'

The Rothschild family is still closely involved with garden management. 'One of the reasons this garden has been so successful is the intimate involvement of the family across generations,' John told me. He meets regularly with the board of directors who consider his suggestions. 'I'm lucky – usually my ideas are approved quickly. The Rothschilds are immediate – perhaps because of their business background. It's very gratifying for me because in gardening waiting too long can mean a missed opportunity.'

Lionel Nathan de Rothschild first moved to Exbury in 1912 with the purchase of Inchmery House, which still stands on the Exbury Estate. He originally envisaged his garden in the grounds there around the house but he couldn't secure planning permission for his design due to a public road near Lepe. When the Exbury Estate came up for sale, he purchased it and proceeded to create the grand gardens known today.

Inchmery was in fact the Rothschild family home until the late 1980s when Lionel's son Edmund sold it and decided to make the house at Exbury the main family home. Today this house has flats in it which are used occasionally by family members and may in future become luxury holiday rentals. Although Lionel was a banker by trade, his passion was his garden, in particular rhododendrons and azaleas. The microclimate at Exbury is ideal for growing these plants.

'He wanted to create a woodland garden on the grand scale similar to what Gertrude Jekyll was doing for the cottage garden at about the same time,' John explained. Some 150 workers cleared brambles, saplings and undergrowth that had taken over during Mitford ownership. Gardeners also double dug trenches to make soil suitable for the grand planting of Rothschild's dream. Pathways were laid wide enough so that Lionel, a motoring enthusiast, could drive among his plants and survey his flowering paradise.

Rothschild planted his garden in an age when plant hunters were bringing back new and exciting species from Asia and this might have spawned his obsession with hybridisation. He was determined to create rhododendrons that were hardier, more colourful and that flowered for longer. 'He rejected species that others might have deemed quite suitable,' said John. One of his great legacies, the fortune rhododendron is large-leafed with huge yellow flowers that appear in mid-March.

This area gets well below the average amount of national rainfall, but it's not something that John is terribly worried about. 'Lionel devised a very forward-thinking system for watering the garden that involved two water towers, 22 miles of underground pipes, and pumps to extract water from deep below the surface. So we've never been reliant on the mains, which is especially important now as the country faces water shortages. We are now working on a system that will harness wind and solar power to pump our water, and are increasingly using technology to make us more efficient. We can record what's happening in the garden on our mobile phones and update our database of plants. One of my great loves, and something the public doesn't see is propagation work, the grafting and nurturing that goes on behind the scenes to fill in gaps.'

The **Exbury Gardens Railway** not only reveals the passion and innovative thinking of Leopold Rothschild, Lionel's youngest son, but it gives a view of the gardens that you don't get on foot as the train passes through areas without walking paths. The commentary is playful and the staff is welcoming – I've even brought my dog along for a ride. In October Exbury runs a special Halloween 'Ghost' train and at Christmas, the Santa Steam Specials can be combined with a viewing of seasonal plants.

The entire estate comprises 2,000 acres of land that borders the Beaulieu River to the west and the Solent to the South. It is worth visiting **Exbury**, a small, linear village built to provide housing for estate workers. Some garden staff still live here but most homes now are privately inhabited. Just past the gardens, the **water tower** was erected to provide water to the gardens. Some of the stonework in nearby **St Katherine's Church** came from a chapel that once stood in Lower Exbury which the Cistercian monks visited from St Leonard's.

⑭ Lepe Country Park

Lepe, Exbury SO45 1AD ☏ 023 8089 9108 ⊛ www3.hants.gov.uk/lepe. Free access.

There is more to do at this coastal country park than just sit on the beach. Low tide gives scope for looking for crabs and tiny sea creatures or bigger wildlife like cormorants and oystercatchers that patrol the mud looking for worms. You can walk out on the sandy spits but be aware of when the tide turns so you can get back to shore. People swim here but the currents can be strong and you have to cross shingle before you reach the water.

In summer this becomes a giant playground but if you visit early in the morning or outside of summer season, you'll be virtually alone. Even on a windy day, you can tuck yourself up beneath the cliff and enjoy the sunshine and drink in the view of the Isle of Wight and one of the busiest shipping lanes in England. Above the beach, the open grassy parkland on top of the cliffs is a particularly good vantage point for observing boats, especially during Cowes Regatta in mid-August every year. Two barbecue areas with sea views are available for hire during the day. They are popular so it's wise to book ahead.

Shelter from the often relentless wind can be found at **Lepe Point**, behind the tall hedges which were planted to encourage wildflowers, small mammals and birds. Lepe Point was just designated a local nature reserve, thanks to efforts by park staff and community members.

The **Lepe Loop** is a pleasant five-mile walk that covers coastline, fields and woods. Pamphlets that describe exactly where to go are available in the café. The off-road **cycle trail** is suitable for families.

Near the visitor centre and café, information boards explain coastal change and Lepe's involvement in World War II when this was a departure point for troops, vehicles and supplies. Still in the water are concrete structures used in the construction of **Mulberry Harbours**, the prefabricated floating harbours towed to France as a means of re-supplying Allied troops. The website has a downloadable audio tour that chronicles Lepe's role in D-day.

The rows of timber groynes that are visible at low tide stabilise the beach and help prevent cliff erosion and flooding. But they are nearing the end of their lifespan and it's possible that they will not be replaced. Experts predict that due to more vigorous storms and rising sea levels, the visitor centre, coastal path and car parks all will be flooded within a century.

⑮ Calshot Spit

This mile-long stretch of shingle beach is a lovely place to walk as long as you keep the oil refinery towers behind you. You can walk all the way to Exbury but you have to cut inland a few times, most notably after Luttrell's Tower where there is a private nature reserve and no public access. The huts at the western end of the beach have been here since the early 1900s when Calshot and Lepe were popular tourist destinations. Today they cost about £20,000 on the rare occasions when they come up for sale.

The rocky **Calshot Beach** is popular with sailboard enthusiasts, sailors and kitesurfers who tend to be more experienced because wind is generated both from the mainland and the Isle of Wight and conditions can get quite blustery. It's a popular place to swim in summer although at low tide you have to walk out a fair way to find deep enough water. There is a place to rent paddleboards and kayaks (*www.24-7boardsports. com*) but in order to hire kitesurfing and windsurfing gear you need to have international qualifications and it's best to call ahead.

On the other side of the spit, towards the power station, is **Calshot Marshes** nature reserve. Birds here don't seem to mind the industrial activity and according to Natural England the site has more than 10,000 waterfowl in winter. The presence of more than 1% of the world population of dark-bellied brent geese warrants this reserve to be labelled 'internationally significant.' It's not the prettiest nature reserve you'll ever visit but there's something oddly inspirational in the contrast between the nesting waterfowl and the industrial site.

Calshot Castle

℗ 023 8089 2023. English Heritage.

You'd be forgiven for thinking that Calshot Castle has disappeared as you drive along narrow Calshot Spit and only see ocean. But keep going and Henry VIII's tower is indeed there, tucked away behind the more recent Sunderland Hangar, built in 1917.

The Tudor fort has been modernised during its four centuries but remains today much as Henry designed it: a central three-storey keep surrounded by a courtyard, curtain wall and moat. A walk all the way around the moat drives home just how small and yet how well-fortified this structure is. Calshot, like other forts built at this time, represents a change in English castle-building with its rounded walls designed to repel newly developed 16th-century cannon artillery.

The entrance is across a 19th-century bridge that replaced the original, which could be raised. On the first floor, the barracks have been furnished as they would have been in the late 19th century when matchboard panelling was installed over the stone walls. The room was only used in peacetime during exercises by the Royal Garrison Artillery. Although it was heated by a stove that connected to the original Tudor flue, it's easy to imagine how cold it might have been when the sea wind whipped around the round tower. The panel behind the stove opens to reveal the original Tudor fireplace and stone walls.

The stairs leading to the roof are steep and uneven. The effort of the climb is rewarded by a sweeping view of the Solent, the Isle of Wight beyond and the colourful beach huts that line Calshot Beach and the vast Fawley Oil Refinery on the other side.

Despite never experiencing gunfire, Calshot is filled with wartime history. For over 400 years the castle remained a fully-manned artillery base. In World War I, Calshot Naval Air Station opened and the site was used as a training base for pilots. During World War II, the RAF purchased Calshot Spit and closed the beach huts. The hangars at Calshot housed and repaired Sunderland flying boats which were widely used during World War II.

As recently as 2011, 87 World War II bombs washed up together on the beach and were detonated in controlled explosions. Next door at **Calshot Activities Centre**, a series of panels in the lobby tells the story of Calshot Spit and its military history.

Calshot Activities Centre

① 023 8089 2077 ⓦ www.calshot.com.

When the Royal Air Force station closed at Calshot, it left some empty hangars on prime coastal land. The largest, Sunderland Hangar, now contains an impressive sports centre run by Hampshire County Council that offers residential and non-residential courses in sailing, windsurfing, kayaking and canoeing.

It's a bit strange to come inside from the windy seafront and see people gingerly making their way down the dry ski-slope that takes up a healthy portion of this huge indoor space. The other popular pursuit here is rock climbing, with all levels of tuition offered, and the chance to negotiate the bumps and hand-holds on one of the biggest climbing walls in the country. You can also take courses from beginner level upwards at the velodrome as well as sailing, windsurfing, canoeing, kayaking and powerboating, and boats can be launched for a fee. Most of the facilities are accessible only through joining a course but if you prove your experience, it's possible to book private group sessions for rock climbing and archery. During winter, there are open group recreational sessions on the indoor ski-slope.

Food and drink

Spinnakers Bar Calshot Activities Centre ① 023 8089 1412 ⑩ www.calshot.com. Beach walkers and sailing enthusiasts come here for the Thai red curry but there is also standard pub fare. The large windows overlook Southampton Water but the choice seating is outdoors in sunny weather. Odd opening times.

⑯ Hythe

Just outside the boundaries of the New Forest on the western shore of Southampton Water is the village of Hythe. Its pedestrianised shopping area has an old-time village feeling and is spared a string of cloned high street shops. There is not much to do other than wander along the waterfront, have a coffee or ice cream and for a little dip into Victorian times, ride the ferry. But isn't that an optimal Slow morning?

The **Hythe ferry** operates regularly all day across Southampton Water between Hythe and Southampton Quay. There is little on the other side (unless you want to have a very un-Slow shopping experience at the Southampton malls for which there is a bus near the ferry landing) but the 25-minute round-trip is a refreshing way to appreciate the importance of Southampton as a port city. The ferry passes the home berths of the big cruise ships, *Queen Victoria, Queen Mary 2* and *Queen Elizabeth.*

It's possible the Hythe ferry might date from AD400 when the Saxon word 'Hithe', meaning 'good landing place,' was used to name the town. The pier, the seventh largest in the country, opened in 1881 and the pier train began running in 1922. The world's oldest continuously operating **pier train** was built during World War I and was originally used in the Avonmouth mustard gas factory near Bristol. That makes it a bit disconcerting, but when you ride this train as it rocks and shudders along the pier to the ferry, you can't help but feel as if you're travelling back in time. Be sure to ride one way and walk the other; the pier has interesting historical placards that you miss if you ride the train both ways. For a small fee, you can just walk on the pier without taking the ferry. For a long walk, try the six miles along the **Solent Way** from Hythe to Beaulieu.

Food and drink

Restaurant choices are limited. If the weather is fine, the best option is to get fish and chips or a sandwich from one of the shops and sit on the grass in **Prospect Place**, a manicured, flowered, waterfront park just beyond the town centre. Alternatively, a short walk from the Hythe waterfront is **Hythe Marina**, a modern development that is soulless but has pleasant views of the marina and Southampton Water beyond. **La Vista**, a convivial café, is popular.

⑰ Eling

In a quaint (or annoying, depending on your perspective) nod to the past, a small toll is collected for every car that passes from Totton to Eling. The Eling Tide Mill's free car park is on the Eling side of the bridge, so you don't have to pay the fee if you approach from this direction.

Eling's history pre-dates the Bronze Age and is linked with shipbuilding. Although it feels like a different world, the town is only just outside the New Forest. Its ultimately Slow attraction harnesses the power of the tide: the **Eling Tide Mill** (*023 8086 9575; www.elingexperience.co.uk; closed Mon and Tue*) is one of the few tide mills in the world producing flour on a regular basis. For over 900 years a mill has been on this site. The present building, constructed in the 1700s, fell into disrepair in the 1940s. In 1975, it was restored by New Forest District Council and volunteers.

As you stand underneath the low ceilings of the restored mill and watch the massive stone wheels turning with the force of the water, you appreciate the effort that went into food production in days gone by. 'Modern flour is ground with cylinders that heat up and effectively cook the flour before it even gets to be used in baking. This means you lose nutrients and flavour,' explained John Hurst, the Senior Mill Assistant. 'We have control over the size of the grain and can tailor it to our customers' needs.' The mill produces two flours, one of which, Flour of the Forest, holds a New Forest Marque because it is milled from grain grown a few miles away in the New Forest. The Eling flour is sold to local restaurants and B&Bs and is available in some farm shops.

The mill only can grind for eight hours each day, four per tide because the mill pond needs to be full and the water on the other side needs to be just low enough to enable the wheel to turn. So if you want to see the mill working with grain in it, you need to check the website or call to make sure all is running according to schedule.

Across the street, the **Eling Heritage Centre** tells of Totton and Eling's evolution since Saxon times. By analysing fragments of charcoal and pollen grains found at nearby Testwood Lakes, archaeologists have determined that Stone Age people lived among willow trees and that the current virtually treeless landscape was created by man over 4,000 years ago. A display about Eling's wartime history features a sound recording recounting its bombing during World War II.

Just by the toll house is an entrance to the **riverside walk**, developed by local councils and volunteers, a pleasant two-mile stroll along a creekside path on boardwalks over the marsh. Walk across the River Test until you get to Eling Cemetery and after crossing through the cemetery and car park, turn right and walk to the top of the hill past the first church entrance. Go up the stairs that lead into the churchyard, cross it, and leave by the gate on the opposite side. Walk down the hill and you will emerge at the field behind Goatee Beach, on the banks of the Test estuary and opposite Southampton's container port, where benches provide the perfect spot to sit and watch the rhythmic, mechanised unloading of ships. Follow the waterside around to the left, past a playground and out onto the dirt track towards the main road. You'll come out at the Eling side of the **Eling Toll Bridge**.

⑱ Testwood nature reserves

Testwood Lakes Wildlife Reserve, Brunel Rd, Totton SO40 3WX ☏ 023 8066 7929 ⓦ www.hwt.org.uk.

Testwood Lakes and Lower Test Nature Reserve are nature reserves managed by the Hampshire & Isle of Wight Wildlife Trust with very different personalities. Testwood Lakes is part of Southern Water's reservoir to supply the Isle of Wight and other local areas. It has a busy **education centre** that hosts school and adult groups. Along with wildlife displays, there are some Bronze Age artefacts discovered during the excavation of Meadow Lake. The building is usually open in the afternoon.

The 150-acre reserve is a mix of lakes, grassland and woodland with surfaced paths and bird hides. It's very popular with local dog walkers and usually busy with families and children. You can have a pleasant short walk around Testwood Lake and Little Testwood Lake on your own or join one of the many organised family sessions that engage youngsters in learning about birds, dragonflies, butterflies and bees. The Reserve is open all year but some paths regularly flood in winter.

Little Testwood Lake is a coarse fishery with rudd, roach, chubb, tench and bream. Day tickets are available from Tightlines Angling Centre in Totton (*1A Rumbridge St; 023 8086 3068*) or Test Valley Angling Club & Southampton Piscatorial Society (*www.tvacspsangling.co.uk*).

Lower Test Nature Reserve (*023 8066 7919; www.hwt.org.uk*) is a much wilder atmosphere frequented by birdwatching groups and serious nature observers. The reserve supports about 500 species of vascular plants, which is about one-quarter of the British total. A very good **self-guided trail** can be downloaded from the website or picked up at Testwood Lakes, either in the education centre or from the outdoor plastic frame. The five-mile walk covers a variety of terrain including country lanes, wooded paths, fields, marshland and, unavoidably, an industrial estate. Part of the walk through this 400-acre designated Site of Special Scientific Interest (SSSI) passes along the 44-mile Test Way, which runs from Inkpen Beacon in Berkshire to Eling. The River Test snakes directly through the centre of the reserve and as you walk through one of the largest reed beds in southern England, you are very likely to find yourself alone with water birds that might include, depending on the time of year, reed and sedge warblers, water rails, bearded tits and sandpipers. It's an odd but strangely satisfying juxtaposition of two very busy worlds. In the background is the ever-present hum of the M27 but at your feet are chirping birds and grasses that gently swish in the breeze. Imposing electrical pylons bisect the marshland yet at their bases in summer, cows graze and birds swoop over the flowers. It's pleasing to see this flourishing hidden world amid a landscape that might easily have been dismissed as an industrial void. Simon King, Reserve Officer, agrees. 'The reserve's location in an urban zone makes it very special. This is one of the only places in southern England where you have the gradual transition from saltmarsh to brackenish grassland to neutral. At most seaside sites you have a sea wall obstructing that gradual transition.'

Several words of caution: because the Lower Test is tidal, footpaths and boardwalks regularly flood. Just before you exit towards the fishing cottage on the self-guided walk, there is ankle-deep water and mud. This

Bracken control

Bracken is one of the most prolific plants in the Forest and can serve as protection for mushrooms, bluebells and wild gladioli. Although not harmful in itself, if left uncontrolled it will crowd out other important species, including heather and grasses.

The National Trust controls bracken using several methods. 'Sometimes spraying is the only effective means, but we are looking for an organic product that doesn't damage the surrounding area,' explained Dylan Everett, New Forest Operations Manager. 'Cutting is effective but needs to be done when ground-nesting birds are not present. Rolling with a machine is good because it bruises the stems and bleeds the sap so that in subsequent years, crops are lower and less thick, allowing other species to thrive. Where possible, we harvest the bracken, bale it, and try our best to re-use it. In the past, commoners used every resource in the Forest and we want to do the same.'

problem should be sorted in the near future but I would recommend carrying or wearing wading boots to be sure. Also, part of the self-guided walk passes through Calmore Industrial Estate. Although it's a harsh contrast to the peace of the wetlands, it is only a short section and very soon you're back in a field.

Lower Test does have a few **organised walks** during the year, usually in spring and summer and a bird walk in winter. There is parking for a few cars in Testwood Lane by the Salmon Leap pub or at Old Redbridges, a lay-by on the A36 between Totton and Southampton. Use these car parks to visit the hide in the south of the reserve. You can also park at Testwood Lakes and walk along Mill Lane, which takes about 20 minutes; this is part of the self-guided walk.

Index

Main entries in **bold**.